GLOBALVIEWPOINTS

Civilian Casualties in War

Other Books in the Global Viewpoints Series

GLOBALVIEWPOINTS

Civilian Casualties in War

Barbara Krasner, Book Editor

GREENHAVEN
PUBLISHING

Published in 2019 by Greenhaven Publishing, LLC
353 3rd Avenue, Suite 255, New York, NY 10010

Articles in Greenhaven Publishing anthologies are often edited for length to meet page
requirements. In addition, original titles of these works are changed to clearly present
the main thesis and to explicitly indicate the author's opinion. Every effort is made to
ensure that Greenhaven Publishing accurately reflects the original intent of the authors.
Every effort has been made to trace the owners of the copyrighted material.

Cover image: ABD DOUMANY/AFP/Getty Images

Cataloging-in-Publication Data

Names: Krasner, Barbara, editor.
Title: Civilian casualties in war / edited by Barbara Krasner.
Description: New York : Greenhaven Publishing, 2019. | Series: Global viewpoints |
    Includes bibliographical references and index. | Audience: Grades 9-12.
Identifiers: LCCN ISBN 9781534503373 (library bound) | ISBN 9781534503380 (pbk.)
Subjects: LCSH: War victims--Juvenile literature. | Civilians in war--History--20th
    century--Juvenile literature. | Civilian war casualties--History--20th century--Juvenile
    literature.
Classification: LCC U21.2 C585 2019 | DDC 172/.42--dc23

Manufactured in the United States of America

Website: http://greenhavenpublishing.com

Contents

Chapter 2: Consequences of Civilian War Casualties

Chapter 3: Civilian Casualties and War Mongering

Chapter 4: Protecting Against Civilian Casualties

Foreword

> "*The problems of all of humanity can*
> *only be solved by all of humanity.*"
> —*Swiss author Friedrich Dürrenmatt*

G lobal interdependence has become an undeniable reality. Mass media and technology have increased worldwide access to information and created a society of global citizens. Understanding and navigating this global community is a challenge, requiring a high degree of information literacy and a new level of learning sophistication.

Building on the success of its flagship series, Opposing Viewpoints, Greenhaven Publishing has created the Global Viewpoints series to examine a broad range of current, often controversial topics of worldwide importance from a variety of international perspectives. Providing students and other readers with the information they need to explore global connections and think critically about worldwide implications, each Global Viewpoints volume offers a panoramic view of a topic of widespread significance.

Drugs, famine, immigration—a broad, international treatment is essential to do justice to social, environmental, health, and political issues such as these. Junior high, high school, and early college students, as well as general readers, can all use Global Viewpoints anthologies to discern the complexities relating to each issue. Readers will be able to examine unique national perspectives while, at the same time, appreciating the interconnectedness that global priorities bring to all nations and cultures.

Material in each volume is selected from a diverse range of sources, including journals, magazines, newspapers, nonfiction books, speeches, government documents, pamphlets, organization newsletters, and position papers. Global Viewpoints is truly global, with material drawn primarily from international sources available in English and secondarily from US sources with extensive international coverage.

Features of each volume in the Global Viewpoints series include:

- An **annotated table of contents** that provides a brief summary of each essay in the volume, including the name of the country or area covered in the essay.

- An **introduction** specific to the volume topic.

- A **world map** to help readers locate the countries or areas covered in the essays.

- For each viewpoint, an **introduction** that contains notes about the author and source of the viewpoint explains why material from the specific country is being presented, summarizes the main points of the viewpoint, and offers three **guided reading questions** to aid in understanding and comprehension.

- **For further discussion questions** that promote critical thinking by asking the reader to compare and contrast aspects of the viewpoints or draw conclusions about perspectives and arguments.

- A worldwide list of **organizations to contact** for readers seeking additional information.

- A **periodical bibliography** for each chapter and a **bibliography of books** on the volume topic to aid in further research.

- A comprehensive **subject index** to offer access to people, places, events, and subjects cited in the text.

Global Viewpoints is designed for a broad spectrum of readers who want to learn more about current events, history, political science, government, international relations, economics, environmental science, world cultures, and sociology—students doing research for class assignments or debates, teachers and faculty seeking to supplement course materials, and others wanting to understand current issues better. By presenting how people in various countries perceive the root causes, current consequences, and proposed solutions to worldwide challenges, Global Viewpoints volumes offer readers opportunities to enhance their global awareness and their knowledge of cultures worldwide.

Introduction

> *"The soldiers of Charlie Company*
> *raped women, burned houses, and*
> *turned their M-16s on the unarmed*
> *civilians of My Lai. Among the*
> *leaders of the assault was Lieutenant*
> *William L. Calley, a junior-college*
> *dropout from Miami ... In testimony*
> *before an Army inquiry, some of*
> *the soldiers acknowledged being*
> *at the ditch but claimed that they*
> *had disobeyed Calley, who was*
> *ordering them to kill ... The truth*
> *remains elusive."*
> —*Seymour M. Hersh,* The New
> Yorker, *March 30, 2015*

Civilian casualties have been a worldwide problem throughout history faced by all sides waging war. Innocent bystanders may be in harm's way or they may be ignored in the name of war. According to Article 3 of Part Four of the 1949 Geneva Conventions, a set of international treaties that protect civilians and wounded military personnel, civilians are persons who take no active part in the hostilities of war. Violence brought against them at any time and place is prohibited. Violence includes cruel treatment, torture, mutilation, and murder.

Since World War II, the definition of "civilian casualties" has broadened to include military crimes against humanity and genocide. Governmental agencies, including the United Nations, and human rights activists have grappled with the task of estimating the number of civilian injuries and deaths.

However, many insist that reported statistics underestimate the damages. Gathering testimonies from affected areas, including the Sinai, Yemen, the Congo, Iraq, and Syria can be vital to assessing fatalities.

One group, the Iraq Body Count Project, maintains a database of civilian deaths that have resulted from the 2003 invasion of Iraq by the United States. The organization gathers media reports, interviews medical personnel, and reviews government records. It estimates, for example, that between 179,000 and 201,000 civilians have died since the United States invaded Iraq in 2003.[1] Such statistics provide data for scholars to model and analyze. There are many reasons, however, for publicly releasing civilian death data. Critics analyze the numbers and determine whether reports drive an agenda or are meant to distort public perception.

When civilians suffer from the barbarity of war, intergovernmental agencies act on their missives to intervene. World War II civilian casualties provide a foundation for international governance to assess and prosecute war crimes against humanity and genocide. The first military tribunal that held Nazi war criminals accountable for their actions took place in Nuremberg, Germany, in 1945. The international law tribunals continue to protect from a headquarters location in The Hague in the Netherlands. Proceedings in 1994, for instance, involved prosecution of those responsible for the massacre of some 500,000 civilians in Rwanda.

Those charged with civilian death offenses can be held accountable outside these tribunals, too. The infamous Vietnam War massacre at My Lai demonstrates how military law punishes those responsible for unnecessary civilian deaths. In this instance, US Army Lieutenant William L. Calley was convicted in 1971 of murdering 22 civilians. He received a lifetime prison sentence until President Richard Nixon reduced his sentence to three years under house arrest.

Honoring combat claims with restitution is an important action. After the terrorist attacks on September 11, 2001, the US Army Center for Law and Military Operations insisted, "[C]ommanders believed that the payment of legitimate claims helped win the hearts and minds of the populace and enhanced their units' force protection postures."[2] More than 500 claims have been made against the United States by families in Afghanistan and Iraq who lost their loved ones.

Government authorities either showcase or downplay the number of civilian deaths, depending on their desire to wage and win war. These authorities may also calculate how many civilian deaths are acceptable. Journalists have reported that these calculations, one of which indicates ten civilian casualties is an acceptable number, are made objectively and impersonally. Some scholars, such as Mary Kaldor at the London School of Economics, argue that the nature of war has changed. She maintains that "new wars" blur the boundaries between war and crime.

International and country-specific regulations are intended to protect the civilian population from harm. Government authorities expect civilian deaths to occur during war. But treaties exist to limit the number of these deaths. For example, the four sections of the 1949 Geneva Conventions and additional protocols were established to restrict the effects of war. In particular, the fourth section protects civilians. It states, "Persons protected by the Convention are those who, at a given moment and in any manner whatsoever, find themselves, in case of a conflict or occupation, in the hands of a Party to the conflict or Occupying Power of which they are not nationals."[3]

Interactive computing scholar Ronald C. Arkin, who authors a viewpoint in this resource, argues both for and against warfighting robots as a means to reduce civilian casualties. Pacifists argue for nonviolent resolution to minimize civilian collateral damage. They outline steps governments can take to lessen fatal effects of war on nonmilitary personnel. However, state resources are necessary for proper training and education to fight terrorism and protect everyday citizens.

The perspectives that follow in *Global Viewpoints: Civilian Casualties in War* highlight the ongoing debates, their origins and potential solutions, exploring and expressing various viewpoints from around the world.

Endnotes

1. Iraq Body Count Project, "Documenting Civilian Deaths from Violence," accessed 23 November 2017, https://www.iraqbodycount.org/database/.
2. Center for Law and Military Operations, The Judge Advocate General's Legal Center and School, Legal Lessons Learned from Afghanistan and Iraq, Volume I: Major Combat Operations 11 September 2001-1 May 2003 175, accessed 23 November 2017, http://www.fas.org/ irp/doddir/army/clamo-v1.pdf, 175-191.
3. International Committee of the Red Cross, "Treaties, States Parties and Commentaries: Convention (IV) Relative to the Protection of Civilians in the Time of War, Geneva, 12 August 1949," accessed 23 January 2018, https://ihl-databases.icrc.org /applic/ihl/ihl.nsf/ Article.xsp?action=openDocument&documentId=78 EB50EAD6EE7AA1C12563CD0051B9D4.

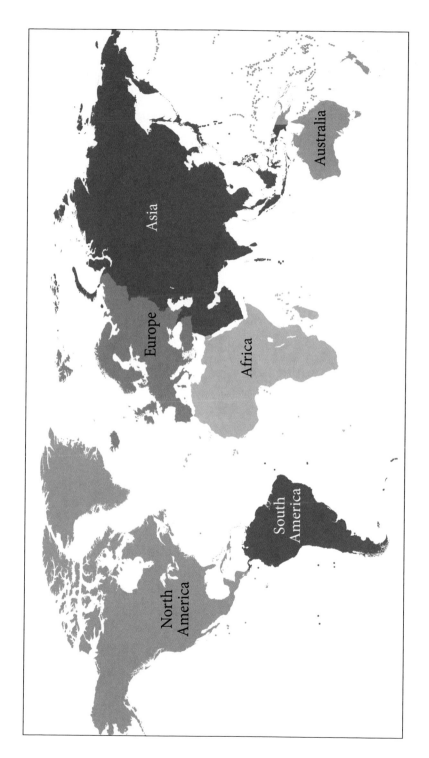

GLOBAL VIEWPOINTS

CHAPTER 1

Civilian Casualties Around the World

In Iraq and Syria, Civilians Deserve to Know Who Is Killing Their Loved Ones

Remote Control and Air Wars

In the following excerpted viewpoint, the Airwars Study for the Remote Control Project argues that the US-led coalition's airstrikes against Iraq, Syria, and the Levant region should take responsibility for the civilians killed in these actions. The study points out discrepancies between its independently tracked numbers and the number of those civilians killed as reported by the military in the US, Canada, the UK, and Denmark. It advocates that the government-issued numbers of civilians killed are not accurate, and it is up to independent sources, such as Airwars and the New York Times, *to report the truth. Air Wars is a nonprofit project that independently tracks and evaluates the war against the so-called Islamic State.*

As you read, consider the following questions:

1. What is the value of independent tracking of civilian casualties?
2. Should governmental authorities share their data?
3. How important is the "right" number to airstrike accountability?

"Limited Accountability: A transparency audit of the coalition air war against so-called Islamic State," Remote Control and Airwars. December 2016. https://airwars.org/wp-content/uploads/2016/12/Airwars-report_Web-FINAL1.compressed.pdf. Licensed under CC BY 4.0 International.

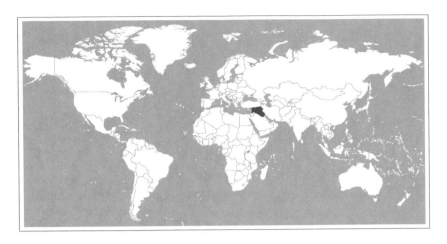

I n recent years, international powers have engaged increasingly in air-only conflicts. The US covert drone campaigns in Pakistan and Yemen; NATO's 2011 intervention in Libya; and Russia's ongoing aerial actions in Syria are all symptomatic of a move towards so-called remote or "risk free" war—with belligerents often unwilling to expose their ground forces to combat. Such campaigns can involve ad hoc international or regional alliances—with each partner nation operating different rules of engagement, and often with wide variations in equipment and capabilities.

The most significant such recent conflict has been the international air war in Iraq and Syria against so-called Islamic State in Iraq and the Levant (ISIL)—which began on August 8th 2014 with US airstrikes on ISIL positions at Sinjar. Since then, at least 16 foreign powers have been drawn into the broader conflict.[1] With so many world powers having carried out an estimated 25,000 airstrikes in Iraq and Syria to summer 2016— alongside actions by aircraft of the Iraq government and the Assad regime—attributing responsibility for any non-combatant deaths is vital.

Yet international powers have adopted radically different approaches towards transparency. While some have revealed the location and dates of all their airstrikes in Iraq and Syria, others including major democracies have declared none. This has significant implications for affected civilians, both in terms of attribution and recompense. At the most basic level, affected civilians deserve to know which nation is killing and injuring their loved ones.

This Airwars study for the Remote Control Project explores transparency and accountability issues within the US-led Coalition. It is based partly on in-depth briefings from senior officials from four sample belligerents (the US, Canada, the UK and Denmark)— and in part on two years of extensive Airwars modelling of the war against ISIL.

The report aims not only to provide a detailed understanding of how such ad hoc coalitions work—but also to identify transparency and accountability good practice for belligerents, and to offer policy recommendations for future airpower-based conflicts.

The Coalition Air War against So-Called Islamic State

The US-led air war against so-called Islamic State has been significant in its intensity. To July 31st 2016 (effectively two years into the campaign) Coalition aircraft had conducted 14,200 airstrikes on Iraq and Syria—with 52,328 munitions released. The US carried out more airstrikes in Iraq in 2015 alone than for 2006—12 combined. Officially the Coalition claimed 45,000 enemy dead for just five losses of its own (a Jordanian pilot and four US Special Forces) by December 2016. More remarkably, it had admitted to having caused only 173 civilian fatalities to November 2016—an unprecedentedly low number for recent airpower conflicts. Yet on the ground, the emerging picture of civilian fatalities proved to be radically different.

By the time the United States publicly admitted on May 21st 2015 to the first two civilian deaths of the war against ISIL, Airwars had already tracked 130 separate reported Coalition civilian casualty incidents across Iraq and Syria. Between them, these had likely killed between 350 and 520 non-combatants according to our own estimates. When the first Coalition deaths were admitted in

Iraq six months later, almost 400 additional civilians had credibly been reported slain.

The disconnect between military counts of civilian casualties and reporting from the field is profound. For the first two years of war, thirteen Coalition nations had between them conceded just 152 non-combatant deaths. Yet to July 2016 up to 4,700 civilian fatalities had been alleged from these same international powers according to Airwars tracking. At least 1,550 of these deaths were likely attributable to Coalition military actions. Overall, it appears that less than seven per cent of civilian fatalities were properly being reported by belligerents. Even in the small number of cases admitted by the US, underreporting of deaths has often occurred. A *Washington Post* investigation found that at least eleven named civilians died in a May 2015 strike in Iraq—mostly women and children—in an attack the US claimed had only killed four.[2]

Relatively high Coalition civilian casualty tolls have also been estimated by others. The respected Syrian Network for Human Rights reports that to mid-October 2016, a total of 649 civilians had been killed in Syria alone by the US-led Coalition—including 244 children and 132 women.[3] A major Amnesty International investigation published in the same month—which featured eyewitness testimony, satellite imagery assessments and munitions analysis—concluded that there was "compelling evidence" to show that 300 civilians had died in just eleven Coalition strikes in Syria.[4] Iraq Body Count estimated that as many as 2,500 Iraqi civilians may have died in the first two years of the Coalition's air campaign in Iraq.[5]

Systemic Military Failings

Conflict casualty monitors are sometimes called upon to justify their "high" casualty estimates. It must instead be for the US-led Coalition to explain why its own casualty estimates are unfeasibly low—particularly when compared with other recent air campaigns.

Since 2009 the United Nations Assistance Mission in Afghanistan (UNAMA) has comprehensively modelled civilian

Civilian Casualties Hit Six-Month Record

25 July 2016 – In the first six months of this year, 5,166 civilians were either killed or maimed in Afghanistan, a half-year record since counting began in 2009, a United Nations report published today shows.

Between January and June this year, the human rights team of the UN Assistance Mission in Afghanistan (UNAMA) documented 1,601 civilian deaths and 3,565 injured civilians, an increase of four per cent in the total number of casualties compared to the first six months of 2015, according to the report, titled "Afghanistan Midyear Report 2016; Protection of Civilians in Armed Conflict."

The total civilian casualty figure recorded by the UN since 1 January 2009 through 30 June 2016 has risen to 63,934, including 22,941 deaths and 40,993 injured.

"The testimony of victims and their families brings into agonizing focus the tragedy of each one of the 63,934 people killed or maimed by this protracted conflict since 2009," said UN High Commissioner for Human Rights Zeid Ra'ad Al Hussein in a press release.

This year's casualties include 1,509 children, 388 dead and 1,121 injured, a figure Mr. Zeid described as "alarming and shameful," particularly as it represents the highest numbers of children killed or wounded in a six-month period since counting began in 2009.

There were also 507 women casualties, 130 killed and 377 injured.

The figures are conservative—almost certainly underestimated—given the strict methodology employed in their documentation and in determining the civilian status of those affected.

In the press release, Tadamichi Yamamoto, the Secretary-General's Special Representative for Afghanistan and head of UNAMA, stressed that the report must serve as a call to action by parties to the conflict "to do all they can to spare civilians from the horrors of war."

Ground engagements continue to cause the highest number of civilian casualties, followed by complex and suicide attacks and improved explosive devices.

Explosive remnants of war disproportionately impacted children who comprised 85 per cent of the casualties caused by such devices. The report contains several accounts of children killed or maimed while playing with such objects.

"Afghan civilian casualties hit half-year record, with 5,166 dead or maimed–UN,"
United Nations.

fatalities from international airstrikes in that country. Its data—never publicly questioned by the US or its allies—shows that even after significant efforts to reduce harm from 2009 onwards, an average of one civilian has died for every ten or so recent airstrikes in Afghanistan.[6]

Official White House data also claimed that in secretive US drone strikes in Pakistan, Yemen and Somalia during President Barack Obama's tenure—an air campaign once dubbed "the most precise in history"—one civilian died for every seven strikes. Public casualty monitors placed that ratio closer to one for one.[7] And thousands of civilian fatalities have been credibly reported as a result of the recent Saudi-led air campaign in Yemen.[8]

Similar civilian fatality ratios if applied to Iraq and Syria—a hot war involving thousands of Coalition airstrikes on urban centres—would lead to expectations of 1,500 deaths or more in the first two years of strikes. This is precisely what the public record indicates.

Why then are military estimates of civilian casualties so low? While there are clear domestic and battlefield propaganda benefits to playing down civilian deaths, Coalition officials insist that mitigating harm to non- combatants has been a key part of their strategy in Iraq and Syria:

> It wouldn't make operational sense to just go into this thing bombing left and right you know—wiping out ISIL at the expense of the civilian population. Because you're not achieving your military aims. So there's a humane aspect to it but also an operational aspect to it, political.[9]

Even so, air-only campaigns appear beset by systemic failings when it comes to assessing non-combatant deaths. Five years on from the air war which drove dictator Muamar Ghadafi from power, NATO still cannot say how many civilians it killed. While privately accepting non-combatants likely died in its airstrikes, officials still talk publicly only of civilians *"inadvertently affected by our actions."*[10]

Outside investigators long ago reached more robust conclusions. As the United Nations inquiry into the Libya conflict noted,

"Amongst the 20 NATO airstrikes investigated, the Commission documented five airstrikes where a total of 60 civilians were killed and 55 injured."[11] A field investigation in 2011 by the *New York Times* also found up to 70 civilians had died in a sample of NATO strikes—including 29 or more women and children.[12]

The reason NATO itself remains unwilling to concede a single non-combatant death from its actions is, according to officials, because at the time the air-only alliance was unable to verify events down below. And in Libya's post-Ghadafi chaos, NATO has never been invited back to fact-check. As one official candidly noted to Airwars, "You cannot determine from the air alone the effect on civilians on the ground."[13]

Yet in Iraq and Syria, this is precisely what the Coalition partners are attempting to do—with participating allies relying almost exclusively on aerial post-strike assessments. It is certainly true that internal analysis has played a crucial role in US civilian casualty admissions for both Iraq and Syria. Of the 62 incidents conceded by CENTCOM to December 1st 2016, 30 cases were never publicly reported at the time as far as Airwars can determine—meaning that the 51 fatalities admitted in these events would otherwise never have come to light. Yet these same air-only assessments also appeared to be missing 1,500 or more additional likely civilian fatalities.

According to the Coalition, each member nation is responsible for the civilians it kills and injures—as well as for the awarding of any *solata* or compensation payments. Determining accountability in hundreds of alleged incidents is therefore vital. For this to happen—and in the absence of trustworthy internal monitoring systems, there needs to be public transparency from each of the participating nations. At a bare minimum this must involve the timely reporting of the date, location and target of each airstrike by its own assets. In addition, nations must properly monitor, assess and investigate possible civilian casualty incidents. As the UN's Human Rights Council heard in 2015, all states conducting strikes in Iraq and Syria "are under an obligation to conduct prompt, independent and impartial fact-finding inquiries in any case where there is a plausible indication that civilian casualties have been sustained, and to make public the results."[14] This study seeks to assess how effective each member of the US-led Coalition has been in fulfilling those obligations.

Endnotes

1. Foreign powers known to have carried out airstrikes in Iraq and Syria since 2014 include the United States, Canada, Australia, the UK, France, the Netherlands, Belgium, Denmark, Saudi Arabia, Jordan, the United Arab Emirates, Bahrain, Turkey, Israel, Iran and Russia.

2. 'A desperate woman's email from Iraq reveals the high toll of Obama's low-cost wars', Washington Post, June 9th 2016, at https:// www.washingtonpost.com/politics/a-desperate- womans-email-from-iraq-reveals-the-high-toll-of- obamas-low-cost-wars/2016/06/09/3e572976- 2725-11e6-b989-4e5479715b54_story.html

3. '649 individuals Killed at the Hands of the International Coalition Forces including 244 Children and 132 Women', Syrian Network for Human Rights, October 21st 2016, at http://sn4hr. org/blog/2016/10/21/28324/

4. 'Syria: Cases of suspected civilian casualties in US-led combined joint task force attacks in Syria since 23 September 2014 [appendix]', Amnesty International, October 26th 2016, at https://www.amnesty.org/download/ Documents/MDE2450372016ENGLISH. PDF

5. Iraq Body Count email to Airwars, July 28th 2016

6. See 'The Strategic Costs of Civilian Harm: Applying Lessons from Afghanistan to Current and Future Conflicts', Open Society Foundations, June 2016, at https://www. opensocietyfoundations.org/sites/default/ les/ strategic-costs-civilian-harm-20160622. pdf

7. 'Do Not Believe the U.S. Government's Official Numbers on Drone Strike Civilian Casualties', Foreign Policy, July 5th 2016, at http://foreignpolicy.com/2016/07/05/ do-not- believe-the-u-s-governments-official-numbers-on- drone-strike-civilian-casualties/

8. Those same Arab partners—Saudi Arabia, Jordan and the UAE - were previously part of the Coalition's anti-ISIL campaign in Syria—where it was claimed no civilians at all were harmed by their actions.

9. Senior CENTCOM official to Airwars, Tampa briefing, May 2016

10. On the record email to author from NATO official April 18th 2016

11. 'Report of the International Commission of Inquiry on Libya', United Nations Human Rights Council, March 12th 2012, at http://www. ohchr.org/Documents/HRBodies/ HRCouncil/ RegularSession/Session19/A.HRC.19.68.pdf

12. 'In Strikes on Libya by NATO, an Unspoken Civilian Toll', C. J. Chivers and Eric Schmidt, New York Times, December 17th 2011, at http://www.nytimes.com/2011/12/18/world/ africa/scores-of-unintended-casualties-in-nato- war-in-libya.html

13. On the record telephone call between author and NATO official, April 27th 2016

14. 'Human rights in the fight against the Islamic State in Iraq and the Levant', Ben Emmerson QC, UN Special Rapporteur on human rights and counter-terrorism, 29th Session of the UN Human Rights Council, Geneva, June 16th 2015, at http:// www.ohchr.org/EN/HRBodies/ HRC/RegularSessions/Session29/Documents/A_ HRC_29_51_AEV.docx

In Iraq, Afghanistan, and Pakistan, the War on Terror Killed at Least 1.3 Million

Physicians for Social Responsibility

In the following excerpted viewpoint, Physicians for Social Responsibility argues that government-reported civilian casualties are understated by at least tenfold. The real numbers rely on government data but are supplemented by eyewitness accounts and surveys. This viewpoint also maintains that the real numbers are less important than the order of magnitude. It is this magnitude to which governments are to be held responsible. It is also this magnitude that should be made public information. The Physicians for Social Responsibility is the US affiliate of International Physicians for the Prevention of Nuclear War.

As you read, consider the following questions:

1. Why is it important to know the order of magnitude of civilian deaths?
2. What value do you think independent university studies provide?
3. Can an actual figure ever be accurately determined?

"Body Count: Casualty Figures after 10 Years of the 'War on Terror' Iraq Afghanistan Pakistan," Physicians for Social Responsibility, March 2015. Reprinted by permission.

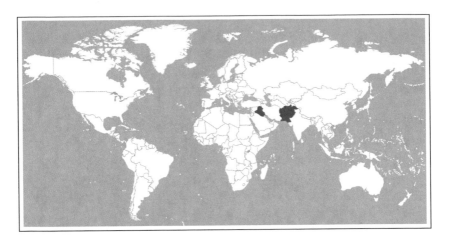

The purpose of this investigation is to provide as realistic an estimate as possible of the total body count in the three main war zones Iraq, Afghanistan and Pakistan during 12 years of "war on terrorism." An extensive review has been made of the major studies and data published on the numbers of victims in these countries. This paper draws on additional information such as reports and statistics on military offensives and examines their completeness and plausibility. It applies interpolation to calculate the figures for those periods for which no information is available. Even now, 13 years after this war began, there has still been no equivalent study.

This investigation comes to the conclusion that the war has, directly or indirectly, killed around 1 million people in Iraq, 220,000 in Afghanistan and 80,000 in Pakistan, i.e. a total of around 1.3 million. Not included in this figure are further war zones such as Yemen. The figure is approximately 10 times greater than that of which the public, experts and decision makers are aware of and propagated by the media and major NGOs. And this is only a conservative estimate. The total number of deaths in the three countries named above could also be in excess of 2 million, whereas a figure below 1 million is extremely unlikely.

Investigations were based on the results of individual studies and data published by UN organizations, government bodies and

NGOs. Figures for Afghanistan and Pakistan are only estimates based on the numbers of observed or reported deaths (passive determination). In Iraq, however, several representative surveys were also conducted in the context of studies seeking to determine the increase in the mortality rate since the onset of war, and therefore the total death toll among Iraqis arising from war or occupation. Although extrapolation of the results of such "active" determination techniques inevitably causes significant breadth of range, this investigation shows that the data it provides is still far more reliable.

Decisive for the publishers of this paper is not the exact number of victims, but their order of magnitude. They believe it crucial from the humanitarian aspect, as well as in the interests of peace, that the public will become aware of this magnitude and that those responsible in governments and parliaments are held accountable.

Iraq

In contrast to Afghanistan and Pakistan, in the case of the internationally much more controversial Iraq War there have been a series of initiatives seeking to calculate the number of its victims. Comparing the different methods also helps better assess the number of victims in other conflicts. Therefore, the Iraq part is the largest one in the IPPNW Body Count. Most initiatives were based on detecting the number of reported deaths, i.e. on a so-called passive surveillance method. Their results vacillate between 110,000 and 165,000 civilian victims of violence, which translates to between 42 and 76 deaths per 100,000 inhabitants and year (in comparison, in Detroit in 2006 the number stood at 48). Moreover, there have been various studies estimating the total number of Iraqi war dead based on on-the-spot representative surveys. Four of them cover a time period until mid-2006 and beyond. Their estimates lie between 151,000 and 1 million, i.e. between 172 and 851 war dead per 100,000 inhabitants and year.

The Iraq Body Count (IBC)

The best known initiative based on passive surveillance is the British Iraq Body Count (IBC). This project tries to capture the casualties of the Iraq War by using a database that counts all killed civilians as reported in renowned Western media outlets or registered by hospitals and morgues. From March 2003 to September 2011, the time period that the present IPPNW Body Count investigates, IBC activists have identified approximately 108,000 killed Iraqi civilians.

Representative Studies Provide an Estimate of Up To 1 Million

Conversely, results from statistical surveys conducted by the Johns Hopkins University, published in 2004 and 2006 in the medical journal *The Lancet*, as well as by the British polling institute Opinion Research Business (ORB) in 2007 suggest that already by 2008 over one million Iraqis had died as a result of war, occupation and their indirect consequences.

The 2006 Lancet Study

At the time of compiling the IPPNW Body Count, the 2006 *Lancet* study was considered the most meticulous of all. The controversies over the number of war dead in Iraq centered on that study. For the study, 1850 households with almost 13,000 people at 50 randomly chosen locations had been interviewed on those who had died during the first 15 months before and during the first 40 months after the start of the war (i.e. till June 2006). The resulting rise in mortality detected from that *Lancet* study allows us to determine the number of dead that occurred beyond those conventionally expected. For no other serious causes come into question, they became direct or indirect victims of war. Extrapolated onto the total population, around 655,000 people had died up until June 2006.

Although renowned specialists of the field, including the leading scientific advisor to the British Ministry of Defense, attested that the study had followed established academic standards, most media had immediately rejected its findings as highly excessive. While projections are commonly used in politics and academia and are widely accepted, in the case of the Iraq studies they were dismissed as pure speculation. Further criticism was sparked off on the authors' alleged bias, the process of selecting the households that would privilege those more at risk (the so-called "main street bias") and the rapidity of the conducted surveys. The bulk of those criticisms, however, as the chapter on the "Numbers War" illustrates, turns out to be either unfounded or lacking decisive relevance.

Comparing the Lancet and IBC Studies

Yet, the numbers cannot be directly compared with each other, because they take a different scope of victims into account. By counting mortality before and after the start of the war, mortality studies try to capture the totality of those who died as a result of war. Initiatives such as the IBC, however, only consider victims of war to be civilians who were directly killed through war-related violence. The same is true with the representative IFHS study of Iraq's Ministry of Health that had merely counted 151,000 victims until June 2005. Through such limitations, not only are combatants not included in the statistics but also everyone who died from indirect fallouts of the war, such as lack of basic health care, hunger or contaminated drinking water. In most wars, that kind of victims exceeds the number of those directly killed. Without detailed on-site surveys, it is hard to reliably determine either whether a dead person had been a civilian or combatant, or the exact cause of death. Regarding all cases of death, the estimate provided by the IFHS study was only 17% below that of the Lancet study.

Extrapolating from roughly 2,000 families onto the total population of then 26 million is, of course, fraught with considerable uncertainty. Yet, the numbers gained from passive observation are not, as many believe, more solid. As experience from other conflicts tell us, only a small portion of the actual number of victims can be captured during times of war. This can also be shown for Iraq by taking samples from the IBC online database.

For instance, the fate of Iraqi medical doctors is relatively well documented. According to the independent Iraq Medical Association, almost 2,000 out of the 34,000 registered medical doctors have been killed. The Iraq Body Count database, however, merely counts 70 killed medical doctors. Often, even US army offensives lasting for weeks, including massive air and artillery strikes on entire urban areas, did not leave a mark in the IBC database. In many cases, there was also no database entry even if there were credible reports from local witnesses on dozens of people falling victim.

When comparing the deaths listed in the US military war logs published by WikiLeaks with the IBC database entries, in both cases tremendous gaps come to fore. Only every fourth entry in the war logs was to be found in the IBC as well, which often concerned cases from Baghdad and victims from attacks resulting in many deaths, where both were using the same sources. At the same time, numerous cases of death are missing from both.

Information on Perpetrators of Deadly Violence

Western media reports heavily focused on terrorist acts of violence, such as car bomb attacks against civilian facilities. These victims are very much represented in the IBC database, whereas those resulting from intense military confrontations—due to the lack of reporting from theaters of war—are barely accounted for. While, according to the families interviewed for the *Lancet* study, at least 30% of murdered relatives were killed at the hands of occupation forces (more than 13% through air strikes), this was the case with only 10% of the victims registered by the IBC (among them 7% through air strikes).

The 2013 PLOS Study

A new study on mortality published in October 2013 in the medical journal PLOS estimates the number of war dead in Iraq at roughly half a million. Its authors applied more refined and conservative statistical methods and, by taking into consideration the objections

Iraqi Civilians

No one knows with certainty how many people have been killed and wounded in Iraq since the 2003 United States invasion. However, we know that approximately 165,000 civilians have died from direct war related violence caused by the US, its allies, the Iraqi military and police, and opposition forces from the time of the invasion through April 2015. The violent deaths of Iraqi civilians have occurred through aerial bombing, shelling, gunshots, suicide attacks, and fires started by bombing.

Because not all war-related deaths have been recorded accurately by the Iraqi government and the US-led coalition, the 165,000 figure for civilians killed from 2003 to 2015 is lower than the actual figure.

It is unknown how many Iraqi civilians have been wounded in the war, though one report states that as many civilians have been wounded as killed.

At least twice as many Iraqi civilians may have died as an indirect result of the war, due to damage to the systems that provide food, health care and clean drinking water, and as a result, illness, infectious diseases, and malnutrition that could otherwise have been avoided or treated.

Several estimates based on randomly selected household surveys estimate the approximate numbers of civilians killed, injured, and made sick due to war. These surveys place the total death count among Iraqis in the hundreds of thousands, including nonviolent or indirect deaths.

Despite more than $100 billion committed to aiding and reconstructing Iraq, many parts of the country still suffer from lack of access to clean drinking water and housing.

"Iraqi Civilians," Watson Institute.

leveled against past studies, they attempted to counter any criticism against their methods from the outset. Thereby, they produced an estimate that can be barely "attacked" but one which is also relatively low.

Despite the discrepancy with the estimates provided by the *Lancet* studies, the PLOS study is buttressing rather than refuting them. On the one hand, the latter's extrapolation far exceeds the number usually cited by the media. On the other, the involved scientists themselves consider their result as an underestimation. One problem lies in the long period that has passed since the war's hottest phases. A more serious problem consists in the more than three million refugees that have not been adequately accounted for in the study—precisely those families who have extraordinarily suffered from war.

There is wide consensus in regard to perpetrators and weapons. While the 2006 Lancet study had only distinguished between foreigners and Iraqis, with the perpetrators being "unknown or uncertain" in 45% of cases, the authors of the PLOS study used a more detailed categorization of perpetrators into "coalition troops," "Iraqi troops," "militias," and "criminals." In 45.8% of cases occupation forces were made responsible and in 27% of cases, militias. Only 16.7% of the perpetrators were considered "unknown."

Taking the time period of the Lancet study, the confidence intervals are overlapping over a wide range. While the numbers provided by the PLOS study appear to be too low, those of the Lancet study can be deemed a bit too high. Therefore, the number of roughly one million victims for the time period until the December 2011 US troop withdrawal unfortunately remains realistic. The difference in the results notwithstanding, the new study reiterates the necessity of statistical investigations.

Afghanistan

There have so far been no representative studies on the number of victims from the ongoing UN-mandated NATO war in Afghanistan. The few investigations that exist on deaths as a result of that war are all based on passive observation.

Professor Neta Crawford from Boston University estimates the number of civilian deaths for the time period until June 2011— on the basis of 14 individual studies conducted over various time periods—at between 12,700 and 14,500. UNAMA, the UN Assistance Mission in Afghanistan, has registered 17,687 civilian deaths from 2007 to the end of 2013. This does not include the victims from 2007, which Crawford puts at 3,500. As a result, we obtain a total number of 21,200 killed civilians until the end of 2013. In average, this amounts to 5.9 civilians killed per 100,000 inhabitants—as such, lagging behind the rate of violent deaths in Frankfurt (Germany) of 6.9 per 100,000 inhabitants.

Of course, the findings from Iraq regarding the ratio between those civilians killed estimated through passive observation and the total number of war deaths gained from representative surveys cannot be transferred one-to-one onto Afghanistan. Yet, they suggest that also here the total number of victims lies ten times higher than the number of registered civilian deaths and may well exceed 200,000.

Regarding the number of victims among those numerous armed groups fighting NATO troops, who mostly are misleadingly referred to as "Taliban," we only have data on a few years. Thus, for the year 2007 roughly 4,700 and for 2010 about 5,200 killed "Taliban" could be detected. The remaining years were calculated by proportionally interpolating indicators on the intensity of warfare, e.g. the annual number of air strikes on resistance positions. In total, 55,000 killed insurgents were estimated. In addition, according to the Brookings Institution's Afghanistan Index and the German government's "progress report Afghanistan" of January 2014, roughly 15,000 security forces were killed between 2007 and 2013—with the numbers growing rapidly.

Pakistan

The war in Pakistan is closely connected to the one in Afghanistan.

The civil war in the Pakistani province Balochistan is mixed with a war on the Taliban whose whereabouts vary between Afghanistan and the north-western provinces of Pakistan. Moreover, supply routes for US troops run via Pakistan and thus become susceptible to attacks there. Furthermore, tensions between India and Pakistan have an impact on the conflict in the regions bordering Afghanistan as well as in Afghanistan itself. From 2004 to October 2012, US drone attacks killed between 2,318 and 2,912 people, a great many of them civilians. However, the majority of killed civilians is likely to be the result of US-supported fights waged by the Pakistani army against various terror groups. In Pakistan, the number of killed civilians and combatants is much harder to determine than in Afghanistan. Even data based on passive observation are barely existent. It can be suggested that at least 80,000 Pakistanis (insurgents, security forces, civilians) have been killed, with twice as many civilians killed than insurgent fighters. Taking all sources and factors into account, a total number of 300,000 war deaths in the AfPak War-Theatre until 2013 seems realistic.

In Iraq, Household Surveys of Civilian Deaths Introduce Controversy

Beth Osborne Daponte

In the following excerpted viewpoint, Beth Osborne Daponte argues that the reliability of two Iraqi household surveys, the Iraq Living Conditions Survey and the Iraq Family Health Survey, has been tested against pre-war mortality rates. For example, child mortality increased during the Gulf War time frame, ending a period of decline. The author considers factors not present in university studies and other independent studies. She also points out the difficulties of implementing surveys during wartime and recommends future action. Daponte is the principal and owner of Social Science Consultants in Connecticut. Previously she worked for the United Nations to evaluate its peacekeeping operations.

As you read, consider the following questions:

1. What difficulties exist to determine the number of civilian casualties during wartime?
2. How important is the way a survey is designed to the quality of its findings?
3. Do you agree that the reliability of the survey data can be tested against mortality rates in peacetime?

Beth Osborne Daponte, "Wartime estimates of Iraqi civilian casualties," Cambridge University Press, December 2007. Reproduced with permission.

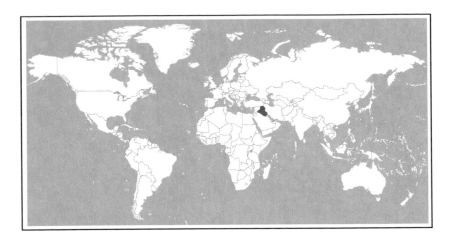

Two large-scale sample surveys have been conducted on the Iraqi population: the Iraq Living Conditions Survey and the Iraq Family Health Survey. The UNDP carried out the Iraq Living Conditions Survey (ILCS) using a two-stage cluster design.[1] The selection of the sample for non-Kurdish areas was based on the 1997 census and for Kurdish areas was based on local lists. In each governorate of Iraq 1,100 households were selected to be included in the survey, with the exception of Baghdad, where 3,300 households were selected. The number of households actually interviewed amounted to 21,668 households, which represents a 98 per cent response rate.

Based on the data collected, UNDP calculated that between the start of the war and the data collection date, which was in 2004, approximately 24,000 people died due to warfare, with a 95 per cent confidence interval of 18,000 to 29,000 deaths.[2] This figure is on the lower end of the 95 per cent confidence interval of 8,000–194,000 that Roberts et al.[3] calculated for the 18 months post-invasion.

The Iraq Family Health Survey (IFHS),[4] conducted in 2006–7 by collaboration between various Iraqi ministries and the World Health Organization, used a design nearly identical to that of the ILCS. The survey's purpose was to estimate mortality between January 2002 and June 2006. A member from a total of 9,345 households in 56 unique strata in Iraq was interviewed.[5] Data from the IFHS yield excess mortality estimates of 151,000 violent deaths since the 2003 invasion and until the survey date, with a 95 per cent confidence interval of 104,000–223,000.[6]

One way of considering the reliability of the data collected by the ILCS and IFHS is to compare pre-war levels of mortality based on these data with the level of pre-war mortality based on other sources. Although the ILCS and IFHS both had a much larger sample size than that of the *Lancet* studies, their results on infant mortality in pre-war Iraq seemed substantially lower than other estimates. The ILCS results show a pre-war infant mortality rate (IMR) of 35 deaths per thousand births for males and 29 for females.[7] The IFHS yields a 2001 IMR of 34,[8] consistent with the ILCS. However, one can contrast these estimates with the 1995–2000 IMR of 94 for Iraq estimated by the UN Population Division,[9] the 1994–9 IMR of 108 IMR estimated by Ali and Shah,[10] the 1999 IMR of 102 estimated by one source at UNICEF,[11] or a 2000 IMR of 38 estimated by another part of UNICEF in 2007.[12] Thus even before the war there existed uncertainty about the level of mortality in Iraq. If results from the IFHS are internally consistent, then one would conclude a substantial rise in the IMR from 34 in 2001 to 41 in 2005.[13]

Similar to the *Lancet* studies, the ILCS and IFHS surveyed households during wartime. However, unlike the *Lancet* studies, the ILCS was careful in its attribution of the root causes of civilian casualties in Iraq. Because of the confounding of other factors at the time of the war, UNDP wrote,

> While the child mortality rate has been reduced in most countries of the world over the last decade, it has increased in Iraq. Exactly how many excess deaths should be attributed to the sanctions and wars is a matter of controversy. Lack of good empirical evidence, combined with discrepancies in the estimates, has produced some confusion. There is, however, no

disagreement that the steady decline in child mortality rates in Iraq in the 1970s and 1980s was sharply interrupted at the time of the Gulf War in 1991.[14]

The authors of the IFHS also provide words of caution in their report, writing that

> Rapid small-scale surveys of households are likely to yield unreliable estimates. Surveys of a large number of respondents with carefully prepared households interviews and multiple methods for collecting data on mortality still run into reporting problems because of the insecurity, instability, and migration associated with the conflict situation.[15]

Other Approaches Possible at a Later Date

Both approaches that have been used to date—tallying and conducting sample surveys—have their challenges. Two other approaches could be used—doing household surveys at a later date, and demographic analysis.

One could wait until after the war has truly ended and the country has returned to a peaceful and stable situation, and conduct surveys on the health and demographics of the Iraqi population. However, asking people retrospectively about occurrences some years prior also has its pitfalls. Generally, responses to survey questions about the past become less reliable as the past becomes more distant. While one would thus suspect that questions about the circumstances of a death may become less certain, the death of a family member may be so traumatic and memorable that the exact date of the death will be accurately remembered by family members, even if responses on the circumstances around the death become less reliable.

Demographic analysis is a tool used by demographers usually to determine the accuracy of a census. However, it can also be used to derive broad estimates of the impact of a war on a population. After fighting has ceased, a census of the population could be taken. If one takes results of the most recent pre-war census and projects the pre-war population forward to the date of the post-war census, taking into account fertility and mortality rates that would have prevailed had the war not occurred and the accuracy rates of the two censuses, then one can arrive at broad estimates of excess mortality by comparing the projected population with the population included in the post-war census. The censuses do not have to be accurate or complete, but the likely degree of their inaccuracy and incompleteness must be known. This approach can yield broad estimates for the country, but usually does not provide trustworthy figures for smaller units of analysis.[16]

Endnotes

1. *Iraq Living Conditions Survey 2004*, above note 3, Vol. I, Tabulation Report, Appendix 2.
2. Ibid., Vol. II, *Analytical Report*, p. 55.
3. Roberts et al., above note 10, pp. 1857–64.
4. *Republic of Iraq: Iraq Family Health Survey Report*, 2007, World Health Organization and Republic of Iraq (Ministry of Health in Iraq, Central Organization for Biostatistics and Information Technology, Ministry of Health Kurdistan, Kurdistan Regional Biostatistics Office), available at www.who.int/mediacentre/news/releases/2008/pr02/2008_iraq_family_health_survey_report.pdf (last visited 5 February 2008).
5. Ibid., p. 4.
6. Amer Alkhuzai et al., "Violence-related mortality in Iraq from 2002 to 2006", *New England Journal of Medicine*, Vol. 358 (5) (31 January 2008), p. 484.
7. *Iraq Living Conditions Survey 2004*, above note 3, Vol. II, Analytical Report, p. 50.
8. *Iraq Family Health Survey Report*, above note 18, Table 25.
9. United Nations Population Division, *World Population Prospects: The 2006 Revision Population Database*, available at http://esa.un.org/unpp/p2k0data.asp (last visited 4 February 2008).
10. Mohamed Ali and Iqbal Shah, "Sanctions and childhood mortality in Iraq", *The Lancet*, Vol. 335, Issue 9218 (2000), pp. 1851–7.
11. See http://www.unicef.org/infobycountry/iraq_statistics.html#27 (last visited 8 January 2008).
12. UNICEF Statistics, UNICEF, October 2007, available at http://www.childinfo.org/areas/childmortality/infantdata.php (last visited 30 November 2007).
13. *Iraq Family Health Survey Report*, above note 18, Table 25.
14. *Iraq Living Conditions Survey 2004*, above note 3, Vol. II, Analytical Report, p. 57.
15. Alkhuzai et al., above note 20, p. 492.
16. See Margo Anderson, Beth Osborne Daponte, Stephen Fienberg, Joseph Kadane, Bruce Spencer, and Duane Steffey, "Sampling-based adjustment of the 2000 census: A balanced perspective", *Jurimetrics* 40 (3) (Spring 2000), pp. 341–56.

In Iraq and Syria, a Change in Place of Battle Puts More Civilians at Risk

Zeeshan Aleem

In the following viewpoint, Zeeshan Aleem argues that the nature of the war in Iraq and Syria is changing, placing an increasing number of civilians in harm's way. He maintains there have been no US policy changes in general and no specific changes between the Obama and Trump administrations. Rather, airstrikes and ground conflict target cities rather than more rural areas. This change in strategy translates to an alarming number of potential casualties with a single strike. Zeeshan Aleem is a political journalist.

As you read, consider the following questions:

1. In what ways can airstrikes on a city produce more civilian casualties?
2. What evidence does the US military provide that it wants to protect civilian life?
3. How do data support that military policy has not changed?

Civilian deaths are surging at an astonishing rate in the US-led fight against ISIS, a tangible sign that the war is growing more dangerous, not less, as Washington and its allies steadily regain territory that had been lost to the group.

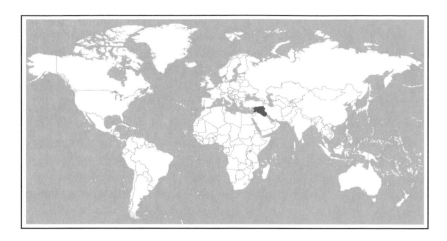

In part, it reflects a major shift in the fight's dynamics. Iraqi, Kurdish, and US forces are no longer battling ISIS in remote and sparsely populated parts of the two countries. Instead, the battle has moved to densely-packed cities like Mosul, where the large civilian populations mean that a single errant airstrike can cause heavy casualties.

And that, tragically, is what appears to be happening. Residents of the Iraqi city of Mosul report that as many as 200 civilians have been killed in airstrikes in their city in recent weeks, including one strike on March 17 which may have taken the lives of more than 100 people in a single blow. If they're confirmed, they would mark some of the biggest death tolls from airstrikes in Iraq since the US launched an invasion of the country in 2003. The US military is now investigating the incidents.

Syria, too, has been hit by US airstrikes with some remarkable civilian casualties this month. A US strike in a rural area of Raqqa province killed up to 30 noncombatants who had taken shelter in a school last week, according to residents' reports. And the week prior, the Syrian Observatory for Human Rights claimed that 42 people, most of whom were civilians, were killed by a US bombing in the town of Al Jinah, in what it deemed a "massacre." The US military said it had a legitimate military target in the area, but noted it would investigate possible civilian loss of life.

The uptick in civilian deaths has been so sharp that it's overwhelmed Airwars.org, a nonprofit that tracks civilian deaths from airstrikes in the Middle East. The site has had to scale back its monitoring of Russian airstrikes in Syria and focus instead on bombings carried out by the US and its allies.

"Almost 1,000 civilian non-combatant deaths have already been alleged from coalition actions across Iraq and Syria in March—a record claim," Airwars said in a statement. "These reported casualty levels are comparable with some of the worst periods of Russian activity in Syria."

US military officials have said they've been working hard to avoid civilian casualties. And, crucially, they've also said that there have not yet been any changes to the rules of engagement—protocols regarding the use of force—in Iraq and Syria, as Trump suggested he would do on the campaign trail. A spokesperson for the US Central Command said on Monday that the head of the command, Gen. Joseph Votel, "is not looking into changing the way we operate, other than to say our processes are good and we want to make sure we live by those processes."

So what's the explanation? There's a number of possible factors, but from what we can see right now have less to do with any observable policy change than they do with the fact that the nature of the fight against ISIS is changing. The easier parts of the war against the radical Islamist group, which has mainly involved targeted airstrikes in less densely populated areas, are no longer the main focus. ISIS's main urban strongholds are now in the crosshairs, and we're going to see more American boots on the ground to help take them. If you're a civilian in these cities, you're in a very perilous situation.

Trump's Airstrike Policy Doesn't Look All that Different from Obama's Yet

US military officials have said that airstrikes are ramping up as the fight against ISIS intensifies in the region. That escalation of strikes, however, doesn't in and of itself seem to be an explanation for the sharp increase in civilian casualties.

Michael O'Hanlon, a senior fellow at the Brookings Institution who specializes in US defense strategy, said that current air campaigns reflect "more continuity than change" from the Obama administration, and that the increase in strikes appears in part to be "the natural ebb and flow of battle, not Trump policy."

That seems to accord with data from the US-led coalition against ISIS. January and February were markedly more intense than the immediately preceding months, but not a total departure from heavier months of strikes during the Obama administration, which began its campaign against ISIS in 2014.

As of now, it looks like March may end up being a relatively light month in terms of number of airstrikes. And yet it's been an absolutely brutal one in terms of claims of civilian deaths.

So what exactly is happening? The fog of war doesn't allow for easy answers, and we're too early into the Trump administration to render definitive judgments about what kind of effect the new president is having on the handling of the war. But one set of plausible explanations revolve around the basic fact that the nature of the war against ISIS is intensifying, and changing in a manner that's more likely to take the lives of civilians.

"The US is moving more into environments that look like conventional warfare, moving up the spectrum from targeting individuals to participating in ongoing conflict, and that's going to produce more casualties," said Heather Hurlburt, a policy director at the New American Foundation and a former State department official.

ISIS has lost about a quarter of the land it controlled in Iraq and Syria in the past year. At its peak, it controlled about 40 percent of Iraqi territory; now it controls about 10 percent. But a great deal of that combat was in more rural and less densely populated areas. Now US-led forces are focusing on urban areas, and the fight to seize western Mosul, a crucial ISIS stronghold, is underway.

"It has been clear all along that the fight for Mosul was going to get harder and harder the further in you got," Hurlburt says. "This is exactly what everybody expected."

Still, the sheer size of some of the civilian tolls suggest there could be other factors at play. "We've dealt with ISIS in urban contexts before and typically we don't have these massive civilian casualty events in urban warfare," says Oona Hathaway, an international law professor at Yale University and a former national security lawyer in the Defense Department's Office of General Counsel.

One possible explanation she points to is the that increased US troops on the ground could make commanders more tolerant of civilian casualties as they make decisions designed to protect growing numbers of embedded US military personnel. In March, the president sent 400 more troops to Syria, which included a team of Army Rangers and a Marine artillery unit, almost doubling their presence in the country.

That trend of troop increases is likely to continue if Trump stays true to his word about ramping up the fight against ISIS. US military officials announced on Monday that the US is sending an additional 240 soldiers to Iraq as part of the effort to retake western Mosul. They aren't expected to participate in front-line combat, but they will be in dangerous environments on their operation.

Both Hurlburt and Hathaway believe that these kinds of increases in the number of military personnel on the ground may change the kind of calculus about use of force that commanders make as they balance duties to leave civilians unharmed against duties to protect their own troops.

It's difficult to pinpoint patterns in the cause of civilian deaths over so short a period of time, and there could be other explanations that emerge for why they've spiked so sharply. The only thing that's clear at the moment is that the war against ISIS is costly for innocents.

International Courts Prosecute Crimes Against Humanity

United Nations

In the following viewpoint, the United Nations outlines the history of the term "crimes against humanity," now governed by international law. The peace organization defines these crimes as acts of murder, extermination, slavery, deportation, imprisonment, torture, persecution, apartheid, and other inhumane acts perpetrated against civilians. It maintains that the 1998 Rome Statute represents the latest mutually agreed upon view within the international community. Importantly, it also differentiates genocide from crimes against humanity; the latter involves no identification of a target population. The United Nations is an intergovernmental organization that promotes international order.

As you read, consider the following questions:

1. When was the term "crimes against humanity" first used?
2. Why are crimes against humanity now under the purview of international law?
3. Is the list of criminal acts all-inclusive? Has anything been left out?

The term "crimes against humanity" was used for the first time in 1915 by the Allied governments (France, Great Britain and Russia) when issuing a declaration condemning the mass

Crimes Against Humanity, United Nations, 2017. Reprinted with the permission.

killings of Armenians in the Ottoman Empire. However, it was only after World War II in 1945 that crimes against humanity were for the first time prosecuted at the International Military Tribunal (IMT) in Nuremberg. Both the Charter establishing the IMT in Nuremberg as well as that establishing the IMT for the Far East in Tokyo included a similar definition of the crime.

Since then, the notion of crimes against humanity has evolved under international customary law and through the jurisdictions of international courts such as the International Criminal Court, the International Criminal Tribunal for the former Yugoslavia and the International Criminal Tribunal for Rwanda. Many States have also criminalized crimes against humanity in their domestic law; others have yet to do so.

Crimes against humanity have not yet been codified in a dedicated treaty of international law, unlike genocide and war crimes, although there are efforts to do so. Despite this, the prohibition of crimes against humanity, similar to the prohibition of genocide, has been considered a peremptory norm of international law, from which no derogation is permitted and which is applicable to all States.

The 1998 Rome Statute establishing the International Criminal Court (Rome Statute) is the document that reflects the latest consensus among the international community on this matter. It is also the treaty that offers the most extensive list of specific acts that may constitute the crime.

Definition

Rome Statute of the International Criminal Court

Article 7

Crimes Against Humanity

1. For the purpose of this Statute, "crime against humanity" means any of the following acts when committed as part of a widespread or systematic attack directed against any civilian population, with knowledge of the attack:

   a. Murder;

b. Extermination;

c. Enslavement;

d. Deportation or forcible transfer of population;

e. Imprisonment or other severe deprivation of physical liberty in violation of fundamental rules of international law;

f. Torture;

g. Rape, sexual slavery, enforced prostitution, forced pregnancy, enforced sterilization, or any other form of sexual violence of comparable gravity;

h. Persecution against any identifiable group or collectivity on political, racial, national, ethnic, cultural, religious, gender as defined in paragraph 3, or other grounds that are universally recognized as impermissible under international law, in connection with any act referred to in this paragraph or any crime within the jurisdiction of the Court;

i. Enforced disappearance of persons;

j. The crime of apartheid;

k. Other inhumane acts of a similar character intentionally causing great suffering, or serious injury to body or to mental or physical health.

2. For the purpose of paragraph 1:

a. "Attack directed against any civilian population" means a course of conduct involving the multiple commission of acts referred to in paragraph 1 against any civilian population, pursuant to or in furtherance of a State or organizational policy to commit such attack;

Elements of the Crime

According to Article 7 (1) of the Rome Statute, crimes against humanity do not need to be linked to an armed conflict and can also occur in peacetime, similar to the crime of genocide. That same Article provides a definition of the crime that contains the following main elements:

1. A physical element, which includes the commission of "any of the following acts":

   a. Murder;

   b. Extermination;

   c. Enslavement;

   d. Deportation or forcible transfer of population;

   e. Imprisonment;

   f. Torture;

   g. Grave forms of sexual violence;

   h. Persecution;

   i. Enforced disappearance of persons;

   j. The crime of apartheid;

   k. Other inhumane acts.

2. A contextual element: "when committed as part of a widespread or systematic attack directed against any civilian population"; and

3. A mental element: "with knowledge of the attack"

The contextual element determines that crimes against humanity involve either large-scale violence in relation to the number of victims or its extension over a broad geographic area (widespread), or a methodical type of violence (systematic). This excludes random, accidental or isolated acts of violence. In addition, Article 7(2)(a) of the Rome Statute determines that crimes against humanity must be committed in furtherance of a State or organizational policy to commit an attack. The plan or policy does not need to be explicitly stipulated or formally adopted and can, therefore, be inferred from the totality of the circumstances.

In contrast with genocide, crimes against humanity do not need to target a specific group. Instead, the victim of the attack can be any civilian population, regardless of its affiliation or identity. Another important distinction is that in the case of crimes against humanity, it is not necessary to prove that there is an overall specific intent. It suffices for there to be a simple intent to commit any of the acts listed, with the exception of the act of persecution, which requires additional discriminatory intent. The perpetrator must also act with knowledge of the attack against the civilian population and that his/her action is part of that attack.

In Rwanda, Crimes Against Humanity and Genocide Violate Human Rights and International Law

United Nations

In the following viewpoint, the United Nations refers to a mapping report that defines and articulates violations of humanitarian rights and international law in Rwanda between the years 1993 and 2003. Specifically, acts were committed upon civilians who were protected under the Geneva Conventions and other international treaties. Affected populations included the Tutsi, Hutu, and Kasaian. The organization lays out war crimes, crimes against humanity (such as torture, murder, and deportation), and genocide crimes as evidence of civilian harm.

As you read, consider the following questions:

1. Were there multiple violations of human rights and international humanitarian law committed in Rwanda?
2. Can crimes against humanity and war crimes be committed at the same time?
3. Which civilian refugees were massacred?

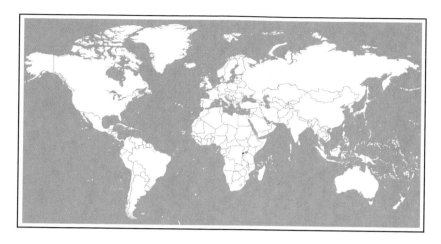

The mapping report identifies the legal framework applicable to the violence that occurred during the decade covered by the report (1993-2003) and draws conclusions on the general legal classification of the incidents or groups of incidents cited. It notes that the vast majority of the 617 most serious incidents described in the mapping report point to the commission of multiple violations of human rights and/or international humanitarian law, which may constitute crimes against humanity or war crimes, and often both at the same time.

War Crimes

The term "war crimes" refers to serious breaches of international humanitarian law committed against civilians or enemy combatants during an international or domestic armed conflict, for which the perpetrators may be held criminally liable on an individual basis. Such crimes are derived primarily from the Geneva Conventions of 12 August 1949 and their Additional Protocols I and II of 1977, and the Hague Conventions of 1899 and 1907. Their most recent codification can be found in article 8 of the 1998 Rome Statute for the International Criminal Court (ICC).

The vast majority of incidents listed in the report could, if investigated and proven in a judicial process, "point to the commission of prohibited acts such as murder, willfully causing great suffering, or serious injury to body or health, rape, intentional attacks on the civilian population, pillage, and unlawful and arbitrary destruction of civilian goods, including some which were essential to the survival of the civilian population. The vast majority of these acts were committed against protected persons, as defined in the Geneva Conventions, primarily people who did not take part in the hostilities, particularly civilian populations and those put out of combat. This applies in particular to people living in refugee camps, who constitute a civilian population that is not participating in the hostilities, in spite of the presence of military personnel among them in some cases." The report notes that almost all the violent incidents listed from 1996 onwards fall within the scope of armed conflict, whether internal or international in nature. "The duration and intensity of the violent incidents described, and the apparent level of organisation of the groups involved, could lead to the conclusion that, with few exceptions, this was an internal conflict and not simply domestic disturbances or tensions or criminal acts. In conclusion, the vast majority of violent incidents listed in this report are the result of armed conflict and if proven in a judicial process, point to the commission of war crimes as serious breaches of international humanitarian law."

Crimes against Humanity

The definition of "crimes against humanity" is codified in article 7 of the Rome Statute of the International Criminal Court (ICC). "The notion encompasses crimes such as murder, extermination, rape, persecution and all other inhumane acts of a similar character (willfully causing great suffering, or serious injury to body or to mental or physical health), committed 'as part of a widespread or systematic attack directed against any civilian population, with knowledge of the attack.'"

The mapping report says that most incidents listed may fall within the scope of "widespread or systematic attacks" characterized by "multiple acts of large-scale violence, carried out in an organised fashion and resulting in numerous victims. Most of these attacks were directed against non-combatant civilian populations consisting primarily of women and children. As a consequence, the vast majority of acts of violence perpetrated during these years, which formed part of various waves of reprisals and campaigns of persecution and pursuit of refugees, were in general terms all transposed into a series of widespread and systematic attacks against civilian populations and could therefore be classified as crimes against humanity by a competent court."

The report suggests that acts that may amount to crimes against humanity were committed throughout the entire 1993-2003 reporting period. Some acts, such as the mass forced deportation of Kasaians from Katanga province in 1993, were committed outside the framework of an armed conflict. Others, such as the 1996-1997 systematic massacre of Hutu refugees, and the murder, torture, and violence directed at Tutsis in the DRC at the start of the August 1998 war, occurred within an armed conflict, and may therefore also amount to war crimes.

The Crime of Genocide

Since it was initially formulated in 1948, in article 2 of the Convention on the Prevention and Punishment of the Crime of Genocide, the definition of "genocide" has remained substantially the same. Article 6 of the Rome Statute borrows from this Convention and for example, defines the crime of genocide as "any of the following acts committed with intent to destroy, in whole or in part, a national, ethnical, racial or religious group, as such." The definition is followed by a series of acts representing serious violations of the right to life, and the physical or mental integrity of the members of the group. The Convention states that it is not just the acts of genocide themselves that are punishable, but also "conspiracy to commit genocide," "direct and public incitement to commit genocide," the "attempt to commit genocide" and "complicity in genocide." It is the specific intention to destroy an identified group either "in whole or in part" that distinguishes the crime of genocide from a crime against humanity.

The mapping report notes that "The question of whether the numerous serious acts of violence committed against the Hutus (refugees and others) constitute crimes of genocide has attracted a significant degree of comment and to date remains unresolved." The report repeatedly stresses that this question can "only be decided by a court decision on the basis of evidence beyond all reasonable doubt."

With that caveat, the Mapping Exercise drew the following conclusions:

- The scale of the crimes committed against the Hutu ethnic group in the DRC, which probably involved tens of thousands of victims, are illustrated by the numerous incidents listed in the report (104 in all): "The extensive use of edged weapons (primarily hammers) and the apparently systematic nature of the massacres of survivors after the camps had been taken suggests that the numerous deaths cannot be attributed to the hazards of war or seen as equating to collateral damage. The majority of the victims were children, women, elderly people and the sick, who were often undernourished and posed no threat to the attacking forces. Numerous serious attacks on the physical or mental integrity of members of the group were also committed, with a very high number of Hutus shot, raped, burnt or beaten. If proven, the incidents' revelation of what appears to be the systematic, methodological and premeditated nature of the attacks listed against the Hutus is also marked: these attacks took place in each location where refugees had allegedly been screened by the AFDL/APR[1] over a vast area of the country. The pursuit lasted for months, and on occasion, the humanitarian assistance intended for them was allegedly deliberately blocked... thus depriving them of resources essential to their survival. Thus the apparent systematic and widespread attacks described in this report reveal a number of inculpatory elements that, if proven before a competent court, could be characterised as crimes of genocide."

- However, the report also points out there are "a number of countervailing factors that could lead a court to find that the requisite intent was lacking, and hence that the crime of genocide was not committed." These include "facts which tend to show that the APR/AFDL spared the lives, and in fact facilitated the return to Rwanda of very large numbers of Hutu, which militate against proving a clear intent to destroy the group." Also the intent underlying the killings, rather than being to destroy the group in whole or in part, could be interpreted as collective retribution against Hutu civilians in Zaire suspected of involvement with the ex-FAR/ Interhamwe, reinforced by the APR/AFDL's conviction that upon destroying the camps, all Hutu remaining in Zaire were in sympathy with the perpetrators of the 1994 genocide in Rwanda.

- Consequently, the report notes, "it is important that a full judicial investigation take place, in order to shed light on the reported incidents" in 1996-97. "Only such an investigation and judicial determination would be in a position to resolve whether these incidents amount to the crime of genocide."

Endnote

1. Given the heavy presence of Rwandan army soldiers (APR) among the troops and commanding officers of the AFDL Congolese rebel group, and the difficulty witnesses had in distinguishing between members of the AFDL and the APR on the ground, the report uses the acronym AFDL/APR to refer to armed elements of the AFDL and soldiers of the APR engaged in operations in Zaire from Oct 1996 to June 1997. Other acronyms in this fact sheet include ex-FAR: the Rwandan army prior to the 1994 genocide in Rwanda.

Periodical and Internet Sources Bibliography

The following articles have been selected to supplement the diverse views presented in this chapter.

Action of Armed Violence, "New Data Shows 70% Rise in Civilian Casualties from IEDs Around the World in the Last Three Years," Relief Web, July 2, 2014. https://reliefweb.int/report/world/new-data-shows-70-rise-civilian-casualties-ieds-around-world-last-three-years.

Scott L. Althaus, Nathaniel Swigger, Svitlana Chernykh, David J. Hendry, Sergio C. Wals, et al., "Uplifting Manhood to Wonderful Heights? News Coverage of the Human Costs of Military Conflict from World War I to Gulf War Two," *Political Communication*, 2014.

Associated Press, "The Latest: Somalia Notes 'Civilian Casualties' in Raid," *US News & World Report*, August 25, 2017. https://www.usnews.com/news/world/articles/2017-08-25/the-latest-us-to-probe-claims-of-somali-civilians-killed.

Thomas Gibbons-Neff, "Civilian Deaths by US-Led Airstrikes Hit Record High under Donald Trump," *Independent*, March 25, 2017. http://www.independent.co.uk/news/world/americas/us-politics/donald-trump-civilian-deaths-syria-iraq-middle-east-a7649486.html.

Jared Malsin, "Civilian Casualties from American Airstrikes in the War Against ISIS Are at an All-Time High," *Time*, March 27, 2017. http://time.com/4713476/isis-syria-iraq-casualties-us-airstikes/.

Ann Rogers, "Investigating the Relationship Between Drone Warfare and Civilian Casualties in Gaza," *Journal of Strategic Security*, Winter 2014.

Betsy Z. Russell, "Frank Church Conference: World Seeing Surge in Civilian Casualties of War," *Spokesman Review*, October 23, 2017. http://www.spokesman.com/blogs/boise/2017/oct/23/frank-church-conference-world-seeing-surge-civilian-casualties-war/.

Richard Spencer, "Civilian Death Toll in Mosul to Pass 10,000," *Times*, August 21, 2017. https://www.thetimes.co.uk/article/civilian-death-toll-in-mosul-to-pass-10-000-8mtpgvpz5.

Yuliya Talmazan, "Red Cross Warns of 'Harrowing' Spike in Civilian Deaths in Syria War," ABC News, October 5, 2017. https://www.nbcnews.com/news/world/icrc-warns-harrowing-spike-civilian-deaths-syria-war-intensifies-n807911.

UN News Centre, "Civilian Casualties Continue to Rise in Yemen, Warns UN Human Rights Office," June 23, 2017. http://www.un.org/apps/news/story.asp?NewsID=57052#.Wj1hHN-nGM8.

Micah Zenko, "Why Is the U.S. Killing So Many Civilians in Syria and Iraq?" *New York Times*, June 19, 2017. https://www.nytimes.com/2017/06/19/opinion/isis-syria-iraq-civilian-casualties.html?_r=0.

GLOBALVIEWPOINTS

CHAPTER 2

Consequences of Civilian War Casualties

Gaps Remain in International Law to Prevent Destruction of Humanity

The Judge Advocate General's Legal Center and School

In the following excerpted viewpoint, authors from The Judge Advocate General's Legal Center and School maintain that the protection of civilians has long been a priority among sovereigns, military and political leaders, religious leaders, and scholars. These stances helped to generate humanitarian law, especially The Hague Regulations and Geneva Protocols. The authors further posit that World War II changed the landscape of war when civilians were targeted. One scholar termed this landscape "an advance to barbarism." Total destruction was now possible. Laws had to be put in place to protect civilians, but gaps remain in international law. The Judge Advocate General's Legal Center and School is operated by the US Army and educates military, civilian, and international personnel in legal and leadership skills.

As you read, consider the following questions:

1. Why did sovereigns want to protect their civilians?
2. What change in warfare did World War II bring about?
3. What recommendations do the authors make to protect civilians even more?

"Law of War Handbook," Library of Congress, 2005.

Introduction

A. Historical Background

The concept of protecting civilians during conflict is ancient. Historically, three considerations motivated implementation of such protections.

1. Desire of sovereigns to protect their citizens. Based on reciprocal self-interests, ancient powers entered into agreements or followed codes of chivalry in the hope similar rules would protect their own land and people if they fell under their enemy's control.

2. Facilitation of strategic success. Military and political leaders recognized that enemy civilians who believed that they would be well treated were more likely to surrender and or cooperate with occupying forces. Therefore, sparing the vanquished from atrocities facilitated ultimate victory.

3. Desire to minimize the devastation and suffering caused by war. Throughout history, religious leaders, scholars, and military professionals advocated limitations on the devastation caused by conflict. This rationale emerged as a major trend in the development of the law of war in the mid nineteenth century and continues to be a major focus of advocates of "humanitarian law."

B. Two Approaches to the Protection of Civilians

Two methodologies for the protection of civilian noncombatants developed under customary international law.

1. The Targeting Method. Noncombatants who are not in the hands of an enemy force (the force employing the weapon systems restricted by the targeting method) benefit from restricting the types of lethality that may lawfully be directed at combatants. This method is governed primarily by the rules of military necessity, prevention of superfluous suffering/devastation, and proportionality (especially as these rules have been codified within the Hague Regulations and Geneva Protocol I).

2. The Protect and Respect Method. Establish certain imperative protections for noncombatants that are in your hands (physically under the control or authority of a party to the conflict).

3. Consolidated Development. Protocol I and IS to the 1949 Geneva Conventions represent the convergence of both the Hague and Geneva traditions for protecting victims of warfare. These Protocols include both targeting and protect and respect based protections.

C. The Recent Historical "Cause and Effect" Process

Post Thirty Years War - Pre World War II: Civilians were generally not targets during warfare. War waged in areas removed from civilian populations. There was no perceived need to devote legal protections to civilians exclusively. Civilians derive sufficient "gratuitous benefit" from law making destruction of enemy armed forces the sole legal object of conflict.

a. One exception: occupation. The desire of sovereigns to minimize disruption to the economic interests with occupied territories mandated a body of law directly on point. This is why an "occupation prong" to the law of war emerges as early as 1907.

2. Post World War II: Recognition that war is now "total." Nations treat enemy populations as legitimate targets because they support the war effort.

a. Commenting on the degeneration of conflict which culminated with World War II, one scholar noted:

"After 1914, however, a new retrogressive movement set in which reached its present climax in the terrible conduct of the second World War, threatening a new 'advance to barbarism.' We have arrived where we started, in the sixteenth century, at the threat of total, lawless war, but this time with weapons which may ruin all human civilization, and even threaten the survival of mankind on this planet."[1]

3. The international response to the suffering caused by World War II is the development of the four Geneva Conventions of 1949, each of which is devoted to protecting a certain category of non-combatants. Although the 1949 Geneva Convention Relative to the Treatment of Civilians Persons in Time of War (GC) is the first "stand alone" document exclusively dedicated to the protection

of civilians, there are obvious gaps in protections for civilians which suggests the victors were not inclined to condemn their own conduct in World War II:

a. The characterization of Allied targeting of civilian population centers as legitimate reprisal actions;

b. Providing virtually no protection for civilians who have not fallen under enemy control.

4. The "Gap Filler." In 1977, two treaties were promulgated to supplement the four Geneva Conventions of 1949. Protocols I & I1 to the Geneva Conventions of 1949 were intended to fill the gaps left by the Conventions. Protocol I for international armed conflict and Protocol I for internal armed conflict. The need for a more comprehensive civilian protection regime was highlighted in the official commentary to the Protocols:

> The 1949 Diplomatic Conference did not have the task of revising the Hague Regulations…This is why the 1949 Geneva Conventions only deal with the protections to which the population is entitled against the effects of war in a brief and limited way…The fact that the Hague Regulations were not brought up to date meant that a serious gap remained in codified humanitarian law. This has had harmful effects in many armed conflicts which have occurred since 1949.[2]

a. Protocol I represents an intersection of both the Hague/targeting method, and the Geneva/respect and protect method.

b. Developing rules based on a combination of both these methods was deemed essential to ensure comprehensive protection for non-combatants subject to the dangers of warfare.

c. The primary focus of this treaty was to fill the void related to protecting persons and property from enemy lethality.

[…]

The Law Which Operates to the Benefit of All Civilians During International Armed Conflict, No Matter Where They Are in the Conflict Area

A. Protection of the Entire Population: Although the Fourth Geneva Convention was the first law of war treaty devoted exclusively to the protection of civilians, only Part II of the treaty applies to every civilian in the area of conflict.

1. Article 15 of GC: Provides for, but does not mandate, the establishment of "neutralized zones" (temporary zones in the area of combat) to shelter from the effects of war:

a. Wounded and sick combatants and non-combatants;

b. Civilian persons who take no part in hostilities, and who, while they reside in the zones, perform no work of a military character.

2. Article 14 of GC: Provides for, but does not mandate, the establishment of "hospital/safety zones" (Permanent structures establish outside combat area) to shelter from the effects of war "Special Needs" civilians:

a. Mothers of children under seven;

b. Wounded, sick, and infirm;

c. Aged;

d. Children under the age of 15; and

e. Expectant mothers.

B. Further Protections of the Entire Population: In addition to providing for the establishment of these "protected" zones, Part II also mandates the following protections:

1. The wounded, sick, infirm and expectant mothers must be "respected and protected" by all parties to the conflict at all times. GC, Art 16.

2. Agreements should be reached to allow for removal of special needs individuals from besieged areas and the passage of ministers and medical personnel to such areas. GC, Art. 17.

3. Civilian Hospitals shall not be the object of attack. GC, Art. 18.

4. Allow passage of consignments of medical supplies, foodstuffs and clothing. GC, Art. 23.

5. Protection and maintenance of orphans or those separated from their family who are under the age of 15. GC, Art. 24.

6. Rights to communicate with family via correspondence. GC, Art. 25.

[…]

Grave Breaches of the Law of War

A. Grave Breaches (GC, Art. 147): Grave breaches, if committed against persons or property protected by the Fourth Geneva Convention, are:

1. Willful killing;

2. Torture or inhumane treatment, to include biological experiments;

3. Willfully causing great suffering or serious injury to body and health;

4. Unlawful deportation or transfer or unlawful confinement of a protected person;

5. Compelling a protected person to serve in the forces of a hostile power;

6. Willingly depriving a protected person of the rights of fair and regular trial;

7. Taking of hostages;

8. Extensive destruction and appropriation of property, not justified by military necessity.

B. Prosecution (GC, Art. 146): Each High Contracting Party shall be under the obligation to search for persons alleged to have committed, or to have ordered to be committed, such grave breaches, and shall bring such persons, regardless of their nationality, before it own courts. High Contracting Parties may also hand such persons over for trial to another High Contracting Party.

[…]

Endnotes
1. Josef L. Kunz, THE LAWS OF WAR, 50Am J Int'l 313 (1950).
2. Protocols Commentary at 587.

In Germany, International Military Tribunals Held World War II Leaders Accountable for War Crimes

Henry Korn

In the following viewpoint, Henry Korn argues that after World War II, the Allies—the United States, Great Britain, France, and the Soviet Union—held Axis leaders accountable for war crimes and the premeditated extermination of Jews. This meant that courts of international law would convene and prosecute such crimes. The first of these was the International Military Tribunal in Nuremberg. Henry Korn is an attorney with a special interest in the Nuremberg trials; he acquired the Nuremberg War Crimes papers of William Donovan, head of the US Office of Strategic Services, during World War II.

As you read, consider the following questions:

1. Why were international laws necessary after World War II?
2. Where was the first International Military Tribunal held?
3. Who established the International Military Tribunal?

Korn, Henry (2017) "International Military Tribunals' Genesis, WWII Experience, and Future Relevance," *Utah Law Review*: Vol. 2017: No. 4, Article 5. Available at: http://dc.law.utah.edu/ulr/vol2017/iss4/5. This article is brought to you for free and open access by Utah Law Digital Commons. It has been accepted for inclusion in Utah Law Review by an authorized editor of Utah Law Digital Commons.

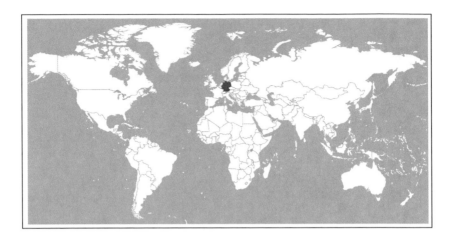

I t is generally known that during World War II ("WWII"), the Allies agreed that following the war, Nazi leaders would face charges of violating international law for the conduct of the war and the extermination of innocent people based on their religious beliefs, and they would face the prospect of death by a military tribunal hearing the evidence. What is not generally known is that the Allies had no precedent for creating an international tribunal and defining anew the very war crimes they would face—an approach that some considered to be ex post facto laws. The International Military Tribunal in Nuremberg was the first time government officials, military leaders, and citizens of a defeated nation were tried under principles of international law in tribunals jointly established by victor nations to hear and sentence the defendants involving crimes that did not appear in any national body of penal laws.[1] This Article discusses precedent, offers personal insights into the proceedings, and suggests the future holds a limited role for such proceedings.

The Allies could have ditched the entire endeavor and lined the war criminals against a wall and shot them. The sentiment offered by Jerome Shaker, a New York City resident, in a telegram to President Truman on October 12, 1946 makes that point:

> Today, Columbus Day, is the birthday of a great, generous and
> proud nation. May I please be permitted to contribute enclosed

check of $10.00 to pay for the expense of bullets instead of a rope for members of the German High Command to be executed at Nurnberg Germany. May God Bless the President of the United States for his generosity in granting my plea.[2]

The Allied leaders had no doubt that targeting German military leaders for all out aggressive war (one of the internationally defined war crimes for the later proceedings) would be judged with skepticism, conflicting with the famous maxim: "war is cruelty," as General William Tecumseh Sherman said 100 years before to justify defeat of an enemy force.[3] As he said, "we can make war so terrible that they will realize . . . however brave and gallant and devoted to their country, still they are mortal and should exhaust all peaceful remedies before they fly to war."[4] To one of his cavalry commanders, he would "propose to leave a trail that will be recognized fifty years hence."[5] He would wage "aggressive war," and "[i]f the people raise a howl against my barbarity and cruelty, I will answer that war is war, and not popularity seeking."[6]

The Allies chose a jurisprudential course for Nazi officials. The United States, Great Britain, France, and the Soviet Union executed the London Agreement ("Agreement") of August 8, 1945 to establish the International Military Tribunals in order to prosecute individuals identified as Nazi war criminals.[7] August 8th was Victory in Europe ("VE") Day, as the Germans surrendered, but the genesis of this Agreement was years before—after the December 7, 1941 Japanese attack on Pearl Harbor, after the Nazis declared war on the United States, before D-Day, and at a time when the outcome of the war was uncertain.[8] The Germans controlled the European continent. Only Great Britain was free of Germany's European hegemony.[9]

The War Crimes prosecutions did not just involve the Nazis; there were prosecutions of Japanese war criminals, although the US chose not to prosecute the Emperor for clearly political reasons.[10] The decision on the Japanese front to selectively prosecute its principal civilian and military officials, excluding the Emperor from consideration and eventually the US decision by 1954 to

---

The First International Military Tribune Put 24 Nazi Leaders on Trial

Twenty-four high-ranking Nazis go on trial in Nuremberg, Germany, for atrocities committed during World War II.

The Nuremberg Trials were conducted by an international tribunal made up of representatives from the United States, the Soviet Union, France, and Great Britain. It was the first trial of its kind in history, and the defendants faced charges ranging from crimes against peace, to crimes of war, to crimes against humanity. Lord Justice Geoffrey Lawrence, the British member, presided over the proceedings, which lasted 10 months and consisted of 216 court sessions.

On October 1, 1946, 12 architects of Nazi policy were sentenced to death. Seven others were sentenced to prison terms ranging from 10 years to life, and three were acquitted. Of the original 24 defendants, one, Robert Ley, committed suicide while in prison, and another, Gustav Krupp von Bohlen und Halbach, was deemed mentally and physically incompetent to stand trial. Among those condemned to death by hanging were Joachim von Ribbentrop, Nazi minister of foreign affairs; Hermann Goering, leader of the Gestapo and the Luftwaffe; Alfred Jodl, head of the German armed forces staff; and Wilhelm Frick, minister of the interior.

On October 16, 10 of the architects of Nazi policy were hanged. Goering, who at sentencing was called the "leading war aggressor and creator of the oppressive program against the Jews," committed suicide by poison on the eve of his scheduled execution. Nazi Party leader Martin Bormann was condemned to death in absentia (but is now believed to have died in May 1945). Trials of lesser German and Axis war criminals continued in Germany into the 1950s and resulted in the conviction of 5,025 other defendants and the execution of 806.

"Nuremberg trials begin," A&E Television Networks, LLC.

---

commute the prison terms of all remaining incarcerated Nazi defendants by 1954, leads to the conclusion that in the end the use of military tribunals to target national figures for war crimes is fundamentally a political consideration which this Article discusses below.[11]

[...]

War Crimes and Procedure

The elements of the war crimes charged against the Nazi defendants thus were unprecedented. The prosecutors were working with new clay to frame the charges within the procedural charter adopted by the Allies. The magnitude of this enterprise is keenly summarized in the October 7, 1946 letter that Justice Robert H. Jackson wrote to President Truman, the original of which is archived at the Truman Library in Independence, Missouri.[42] As Justice Jackson advised President Truman:

- The first trial of Nazi governmental officials and military leaders began on November 20, 1945 and occupied 216 trial days.

- 33 witnesses were called by the prosecution and subject to defense attorneys' cross examination.

- The defense attorneys called 61 witnesses and 19 of the 22 defendants testified in their defense.

- 143 other witnesses called by the defense attorneys gave testimony through written interrogatories.

- The proceedings were conducted and recorded in 4 languages, English, German, French, and Russian, and daily transcripts in the language of the choice of the attorneys were prepared.[43]

- The English transcript covered over 17,000 pages.

- For the trial preparation, Justice Jackson stated that over 100,000 captured German documents were screened and examined and about 4,000 were translated into the 4 languages and used in whole or in part at the trial and marked as trial exhibits.

- Of the millions of feet of captured film, over 100,000 feet were presented at trial as exhibits.

- Over 25,000 photographs were examined by the prosecution and more than 1,800 were trial exhibits, and Hitler's photographer was a prosecution witness who authenticated the photographs.

- Justice Jackson also summarized the administrative aspects of trial preparation and trial, stating that the US staff directly engaged in the trial included 654 lawyers, secretaries, translators, interpreters and clerical staff. 365 of the foregoing were civilians.

- The press and radio had a maximum of 249 accredited representatives.

- The courthouse in Nuremburg was a bombed shell and had to undergo extensive repairs before proceedings could be held.

- The courthouse kitchen served over 1,500 lunches on court days.[44]

The take-away from the Nuremberg War Crimes initial trial of leading governmental officials and military leaders,[45] including Hermann Goering (head of the German air force and principal Nazi official below Adolph Hitler to head the German government), Joachim von Ribbentrop, Nazi foreign minister, and Admiral Erich Raeder and Karl Donitz, chiefs of German naval forces, is clearly spelled out in Chief Prosecutor Robert H. Jackson's October 7, 1946 letter to President Harry Truman.[46] That letter, and a treasure trove of other correspondence and documents on the war crimes proceedings, is part of the archives of the Truman Library.[47]

Writing about the conviction and sentencing of 19 of the 22 defendants in this trial, Justice Jackson highlighted the four principles that were set by these proceedings, stating:

> The vital question in which you and the country are interested is whether the results of this trial justify this heavy expenditure of effort. While the sentences imposed upon individuals hold dramatic interest, and while the acquittals, especially of Schact and Von Papen, are regrettable, the importance of this case is not measurable in terms of the personal fate of any of the defendants who were already broken and discredited men. We are too close to the trial to appraise its long-range effects. The

only criterion of success presently applicable is the short-range test as to whether we have done what we set out to do. This was outlined in my report to you on June 7, 1945. By this standard we have succeeded.

Endnotes

1. See The Trial of German Major War Criminals, Proceedings of the International Military Tribunal Sitting at Nuremberg, Germany 1, 49–50 (1945) [hereinafter Proceedings] (quoting Justice Robert Jackson as saying "The privilege of opening the first trial in history for crimes against the peace of the world imposes a grave responsibility."); see also TELFORD TAYLOR, ANATOMY OF THE NUREMBERG TRIALS 47 (1st ed., 1972).

2. Telegram from Jerome Shaker to Harry S. Truman on Oct. 12, 1946, HARRY S. TRUMAN: LIBRARY & MUSEUM, https://www.trumanlibrary.org/ whistlestop/study_ collections/nuremberg/documents/index.php?documentid=2-9&pagenumber=1 [https://perma.cc/FBW8-KNHW].

3. Letter of William T. Sherman to James M. Calhoun, E.E. Rawson, and S.C. Wells, September 12, 1864, CIVIL WAR ERA NC, http://cwnc.omeka.chass.ncsu.edu/items/ show/23 [https://perma.cc/G3TM-7PUB].

4. Letter from William T. Sherman to Ellen Ewing Sherman (October 22, 1862), in THE SHERMAN LETTERS: CORRESPONDENCE BETWEEN GENERAL AND SENATOR SHERMAN FROM 1837 TO 1891 (ed. Rachel Sherman Thorndike, 1894).

5. WILLIAM TECUMSEH SHERMAN, MEMOIRS OF GENERAL W. T. SHERMAN 38 (2010).

6. Id. at 38–39.

7. Proceedings, supra note 1, at 1.

8. The initial decision of the Allies to convene an international military tribunal to prosecute the Nazi leaders was made in October 1943, over 9 months before the Allies landed at Normandy to liberate Europe from Nazi domination. Clearly, Germany controlled Europe when the Allies conceived the war crimes tribunals as the modality to deal with the Nazi officials when war came to an end.

9. In a resolution dated October 10, 1943, the Executive Committee of the League of Nations Union announced that individuals, including governmental officials, military officials and industrialists, in Germany should be prosecuted by international military tribunals for war crimes, including a system of terror by slaughter and torture, "unjustified by any military necessity and aimed at men, women and children of all ages and in certain cases dictated by racial or religious prejudice as in the wholesale massacre of Jews." Statement, Punishment and Prevention of War Crimes, Resolution of the Executive Committee of the League of Nations Union, October 10, 1943, HARRY S. TRUMAN: LIBRARY & MUSEUM, https://www. trumanlibrary.org/whistlestop/study_collections/nuremberg/docu ments/index. php?documentdate=1943-10-10&documentid=C107-10-2&pagenumber=1 [https:// perma.cc/573N-SXV4].

10. H.W. BRANDS , THE GENERAL VS . THE PRESIDENT : MAC ARTHUR AND TRUMAN AT THE BRINK OF NUCLEAR WAR 19–20 (2016).

11. The decision of then Secretary of State John J. McCloy, with the support of President Eisenhower, to commute the prison terms of the Nazi officials was part of the U.S. effort to reintegrate Germany into a European force to confront the Soviet Union

during the Civil War. See id. at 9; see also TAYLOR , supra note 1, at 640.

42. The author visited the Truman Library on October 30, 2016 and was permitted to access all relevant documents involving the origins of, war crimes charges, and procedure, and viewpoints expressed by senior government officials, including President Truman, about these proceedings.

43. The author and his wife in 1998 acquired the entire private collection of trial transcripts and investigative materials assembled by William Donovan, Director of the Office of Strategic Services, and donated the Donovan Collection to Cornell University, where they are available to the public through Cornell's library website at lawcollections.library.cornell.edu/nuremberg. Issues involving the conflict between General Donovan and Justice Jackson (clearly very strong personalities) over the manner in which evidence should be presented at the trials, including use of defendants as witnesses testifying pursuant to cooperation agreements, eventually led to Donovan's resigning from participation as lead investigator, the details of which are found in a series of interesting letters between Donovan and Jackson and President Truman, and which are also archived in the Truman Library. *See* discussion *infra* Section IV (discussing the Donovan/Jackson conflict).

44. Report to the President by Mr. Justice Jackson, Oct. 7, 1946, *in* International Conference on Military Trials, London, 1945 [hereinafter Justice Jackson Letter], http://avalon.law.yale.edu/imt/jack63.asp [https://perma.cc/5PUX-KCWB].

45. In addition to the trial of the major Nazi war criminals that covered the period of November 20, 1945 through October 1, 1946, there were 12 other trials of Nazi war criminals. *See* Telford Taylor, Final Report to the Secretary of the Army on the Nuremberg War Crimes Trials Under Control Council Law No. 10, Memorandum for the Secretary of War, at 36 (1946) [hereinafter Taylor Memorandum]. The chief prosecutor of the first trial involving senior governmental officials and military leaders was Robert H. Jackson, who before his tenure as trial counsel representing the United States was a Justice of the U.S. Supreme Court. Id. at 22. General Telford Taylor succeeded Justice Jackson and was chief counsel of the remaining 12 separate trials. Id. at 259. Only Jackson prosecuted major Nazi war criminals who were tried before the International Military Tribunal, and whose jurists were selected from each of the Allied countries. See id. at 10–11. The remaining 12 trials were conducted before U.S. military tribunals, also in the same courthouse as the first trial, and those 12 trials covered the period December 9, 1946 through December 1948. See id.

46. Justice Jackson Letter, supra note 44.

47. Public Papers of the Presidents: Harry S. Truman 1945-1953, HARRY S. TRUMAN LIBRARY & MUSEUM, https://www.trumanlibrary.org/publicpapers/index.php [https://perma.cc/CR8N-RL59].

In Afghanistan and Iraq, the Foreign Claims Act Is Not Enough to Compensate Civilian Casualties

Jonathan Tracy

In the following excerpted viewpoint, Jonathan Tracy argues that despite claims made through the Foreign Claims Act, Afghan and Iraqi families do not receive the compensation they seek for the loss of their nonmilitary loved ones caused by US service members. Tracy cites the claims of 506 cases as representative of the more than tens of thousands of cases made. He maintains that the payment process is neither well understood nor adequately utilized. He also presents recommendations to rectify the problem. Jonathan Tracy is a retired army captain and lawyer. He served as a consultant for the Campaign for Innocent Victims in Conflict.

As you read, consider the following questions:

1. Through which act and which program can Iraqi and Afghan families file claims to receive compensation for the death of their loved ones?
2. What needs to happen for the better utilization of this act and program?
3. What is the benefit of a more fair and equitable use of this act and program?

"Compensating Civilian Casualties: 'I am sorry for your loss and I wish you well in a free Iraq,'" by Jonathan Tracy, Center for Civilians in Conflict (CIVIC), May 30, 2008. Reprinted by permission.

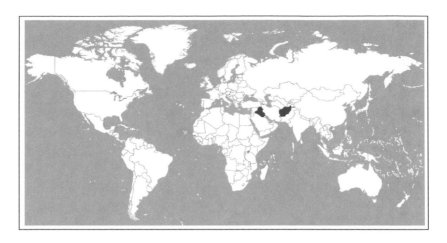

On November 12, 2004, US soldiers and anti-Iraqi forces battled on the streets of Hawija, Iraq.[1] An innocent Iraqi civilian, standing at the front gate to his family's property when the firefight began, was killed in the crossfire. Several months later, the victim's brother filed a claim for compensation under the Foreign Claims Act with the judge advocate at the 116th Brigade Combat Team, 42nd Infantry Division. The judge advocate denied the claim. A denial letter explained the decision: "The US cannot pay your claim because your brother's death was incident to combat. I am sorry for your loss, and I wish you well in a Free Iraq."[2] Yet, in a symbolic gesture, the judge advocate approved a condolence payment in the amount of $500 for the victim's family "as an expression of sympathy and good will and in the best interest of the US government."[3] Tens of thousands of similar cases have been decided in Afghanistan and Iraq since 2002. This is an under-examined element to US armed conflicts. The public and military experts understand the reality facing civilians in a combat zone, but few wonder how the military helps individual victims after harm occurs.

The "center of gravity" in counterinsurgency campaigns is the civilian population and US military counterinsurgency doctrine focuses strategists' primary attention on "securing the civilian" rather than "destroying the enemy."[4] In such operational environments, civilian casualties are not viewed merely as "unintended consequences" that result in "collateral damage." Instead, gaining civilian support after, and despite, instances of civilian casualties becomes a vital strategic goal. Two programs help achieve this goal in Afghanistan and Iraq: the Foreign Claims Act (FCA) and the condolence payment program. These programs are not new; however, for the first time, the public now has access to numerous cases decided in Afghanistan and Iraq. These files provide insight into both the nature of the fighting in Afghanistan and Iraq and how well the US military helps people after causing civilian casualties.

The FCA authorizes compensation awards to foreign nationals for death, injury and damage to property from "noncombat activity or a negligent or wrongful act or omission" caused by US service members.[5] The condolence payment program, separately, is part of the Commander's Emergency Response Program fund and authorizes commanders to provide symbolic "gifts" for death, injury, or battle damage caused during US military combat operations.[6] Various sources indicate that approximately $30-35 million in Foreign Claims Act awards and $40-45 million in condolence payments have been made in Afghanistan and Iraq since 2002.[7] Both programs are ex gratia (an "act of grace"), meaning no law requires an award or payment. However, many military planners understand the strategic imperative in using these programs to gain civilian support. Similar programs date back to World War I in US military history. Yet, the American public, the Iraqi and Afghan people, and major segments of the US military do not adequately understand these programs.

This report examines 506 claims filed by Afghan and Iraqi civilians against the US military for monetary aid for harm allegedly caused by US forces. Tens of thousands of such claims have been filed in Afghanistan and Iraq; however, the 506 claims researched for this report represent the only files released by the US government to date. The American Civil Liberties Union (ACLU) received these documents pursuant to a Freedom of Information

Act (FOIA) request.[8] The files account for close to 2,000 pages.

The cases examined indicate that the FCA and the condolence payment program are not being utilized appropriately. If steps are taken to improve these programs, the military will be better able to respond to civilian harm and better meet its strategic objectives. Military doctrine and training properly stresses the need to limit civilian casualties. However, zero civilian casualties in a combat zone will always remain impossible. A fair and equitable FCA system and condolence payment program will help ameliorate animosity toward the US military after civilian casualties occur.

While the strategic interests involved should be enough to influence military planners to improve these programs, it is essential to remember that these claims affect people's lives and livelihoods. Militaries should attempt to help where they have harmed to lessen civilian suffering. Therefore, the goal must be to utilize the FCA and the condolence payment program to gain the trust and support of the civilian populations and victims and survivors recover after harm occurs.

[…]

Recommendations

Each of the problems discussed in the preceding part of this report can be overcome. The solutions offered here can be accomplished within the existing structure of the two programs. They will not solve every problem associated with the FCA and the condolence payment program, but they would solve all the ones highlighted in this report that were evident in the files released. Further structural changes could be implemented to ensure greater success in gaining the trust and confidence of the civilian populations and thereby helping the military meet certain strategic objectives. Those are not outlined here. While the recommendations here will not create a perfect system, they would improve the current system without any structural changes to the military claims system.

1. Improve training opportunities for judge advocates on the Foreign Claims Act:

One of the problems uncovered in the above sections is that judge advocates appear hesitant to issue awards under the FCA when negligence of US service members may be at issue. For example, in the few instances where service members did act negligently by firing too many rounds or not properly identifying a target before firing, a judge advocate above the rank of captain issued the decision. Quite possibly the younger judge advocates do not understand the nuances of the law and regulations well enough to make informed and reasoned decisions. Instead of approving an award they would rather deny claims under the easy banner of the "combat exclusion." Most judge advocates serving as foreign claims commissioners at the brigade and division levels are captains and it would not be feasible to assign more senior officers to those positions. Therefore, more extensive training could help give the judge advocates the confidence and knowledge to adjudicate these cases properly and in accordance with the law. Providing with a slightly longer period during officer basic course dedicated to combat claims and by offering more continued legal education trainings before deployments could do this.

Increased training will ensure that claims will be adjudicated properly. For instance, the "combat exclusion" will not be the presumed conclusion for most claims, facts will be analyzed against the law and regulations, case-by-case determinations will be issued, amounts awarded will be fair and reasonable, inappropriate standards of proof will not be followed, unacceptable determinations on the value of certain evidence will be avoided, and continuity in the program will extend across a deployment area.

2. Require detailed legal analysis in all Foreign Claims Act memorandums and decisions:

One of the most disappointing aspects of the released files is the utter lack of legal analysis in the memorandums of opinion. The judge advocates serving as foreign claims commissioners are adjudicating legal claims. They must approach this duty knowing that their responsibility as licensed attorneys requires them to make reasoned decisions. Emphasis must be made in the training of foreign claims commissioners and direction must come from their senior officers in the field to perform their legal obligation by providing competent and legal decisions in every case.

3. Require more continuity in awards under the Foreign Claims Act:

When some local nationals receive an award in a certain type of case and their neighbor does not, and when some local nationals receive higher awards than others for substantially the same harm, animosity among the civilian population will likely rise. Therefore, it is in the interests of the US military to ensure that similar cases be adjudicated similarly. Obviously, certain facts may require differences and cases should be decided on a case-by-case basis. However, wide disparities must be avoided. Certain insurance industries utilize various matrixes for determining damages. This would be appropriate in combat claims so long as there is still some room for judge advocates to adjust certain awards in specific cases.

4. Improve training opportunities for judge advocates, civil affairs officers, and commanders on the condolence payment program:

The condolence payment program is a powerful tool at the hands of a brigade or division. It holds the potential to increase the civilian population's support for the military in dramatic ways. The program is not as legalistic as the FCA system and is designed to be used quickly and without prohibitive barriers. But to use the program effectively, the unit must enact a comprehensive program at various levels to ensure all potential victims receive a payment in a timely fashion. Judge advocates, civil affairs and commanders all have the potential of meeting civilian casualties and need to know how to expedite valid claims through the system. If a FCA claim is denied under the "combat exclusion" and the victim was not an enemy of the US, a payment should be offered at the earliest possible moment.

This training would be best served if it comes during a unit's pre-deployment exercises at combat training centers and during class sessions at the unit's home station. During the unit's deployment to a combat training center (like the National Training Center at Fort Irwin) training scenarios should include combat claims and require units to walk civilian actors through the condolence payment program. During class room sessions at the unit's home station, a combat claims expert should detail different systems the unit should follow in the field to ensure the successful implementation of the program.

5. Incorporate the claims and condolence payment missions at all levels within a unit:

As discussed above, many claims did not receive an FCA award because of a lack of evidence. However, the analysis also demonstrated that SIGACTs are less than perfect. It appears that many cases could have received compensation if the unit recorded all instances of potential civilian casualties. Units should designate unit claims officers and empower them with authority to demand evidence and information regarding all potential instances of civilian casualties. Further, commanders must instill in soldiers the need and obligation to report all situations that may result in civilian casualties, whether from a vehicle accident or a firefight. The military must make capturing information surrounding civilian casualties caused by US forces a top priority. Software programs exist that would enable this information to be captured easily and stored in a usable manner. Units and soldiers are already required to capture certain types of information, adding a requirement about civilian casualties would be a minimum burden and offer great benefits by increasing the military's chances for helping where it has harmed.

6. Distill lessons learned from appropriate cases to improve escalation of force and rules of engagement training:

A majority of the 506 cases resulted from incidents where the harm occurred during an event known as an escalation of force incident. This means US personnel perceived a threat and tried to neutralize that threat through a series of graduated response measures. In almost every case the perceived threat was not substantiated. Training of commanders and soldiers is extensive in this area before units deploy. Clearly, the military would do well to capture the information in all claims files dealing with an escalation of force event to draw lessons learned to determine how well soldiers implement their training and to determine if the training is adequate or needs changing.

Consider a few cases. In one, US forces shot and killed the claimant's son when a convoy approached the victim's car from the rear.[193] A SIGACT explained that the son failed to yield to the convoy after proper warnings were issued. Next, a warning shot was fired and the victim slowed down. Fearing the vehicle was blocking the patrol into a complex IED attack, the patrol leader fired another shot into the cab of the vehicle. It appears at first the convoy wanted the driver to yield and when he did slow down they thought he was setting up an attack. Is this a reasonable use of force? Could trainers use this fact pattern to determine if a better approach could have been utilized? Nothing linked the man to the insurgency since no contraband was found in the vehicle.

In a second case, US soldiers guarding an election site engaged a vehicle that seemed suspicious.[194] According to a SIGACT the US used VS-17 panels, flashlights, and hand and arm signals to stop the vehicle. The driver claimed he did not see the light or the hand signals employed by US soldiers. One passenger was killed and another injured. Were the lights and signals powerful enough? Should the unit revisit its systems to see what could be improved? How quickly can a soldier resort to force? These important lessons can be gleaned by examining these types of cases.

In another case, US forces killed the claimant's brother.[195] Allegedly, the brother pulled over to the side of the road to fix his vehicle. The US service members involved claim that the victim made eye contact with the patrol as it passed, he then picked up a long cylindrical object and began to run. The soldiers also claim the vehicle began to move. US forces fired "multiple warning shots before the vehicle stopped."[196] The SIGACT excerpt reads: "Patrol did not discover any AIF [anti-Iraqi forces] related equipment."[197] Could different means have been used? Did the victim run because of the threat posed by US forces? What could have been done differently?

This lesson is not lost on members of the military. Training on the use of force must include an understanding of how local nationals will likely react to US forces in given circumstances. Simply expecting civilians unfamiliar with US troops to obey commands perfectly is unreasonable.

For example, in one case, the claimant's father was warned to pull over by a US convoy and then shot when he did not.[199] A SIGACT revealed that "Instead of pulling over to the side of the road, the deceased turned his lights on high and continued down the road toward the convoy. One warning shot was fired which caused the vehicle to depart the roadway."[200] Nothing was found linking the victim to the insurgency. Is it not unreasonable for a driver to put on high beams when a truck approaches? Were his actions unreasonable or should the military reexamine how convoys travel on roads?

There was one example where the unit did use the incident to evaluate their processes.[201] They conducted an Army Regulation 15-6 investigation into an escalation of force event. According to the file, a "convoy observed a vehicle in the opposite lane pull out from a line of stopped vehicles and accelerated towards the convoy. The gunner (SPC [REDACTED]) waved a chemical light at the vehicle and then threw the chemical light towards the vehicle in an effort to alert the driver."[202] The victim did not stop and the gunner opened fire. The Army Regulation 15-6 investigation concluded that the shooter should not face any criminal charges but that "[r]etraining is appropriate under these circumstances."[203] The investigator also recommended that "the Battalion [review], and if necessary [revise] its standards for engagement criteria to include lessons learned from this incident."[204]

Such thorough examinations should be conducted in all such cases to ensure the military does all it can to limit civilian casualties, not simply out of moral considerations, but because it is in their strategic self-interest. Clearly, the tools available to inspect situations in a non-combat zone versus a combat zone vary greatly. But every effort should be made to try and understand what happened, to determine if any important lessons learned can be drawn from the use of force in a given situation and to provide some help to all innocent civilian casualties.

7. Release all claims documents:

The 506 cases analyzed for the purposes of this report provide an important start to assessing the use of these programs. However, a more thorough examination is necessary. It is in the interest of the US military to draw lessons learned from all of the claims files brought by Afghan and Iraqi civilians. This will help the military do a better job in the current conflicts and in future engagements. To date, requests by various civil society organizations have met with very limited success. The US government should release all of the claims documents with appropriate redactions as early as possible.

Endnotes

1. See http://www.aclu.org/natsec/foia/pdf/Army0268_0270.pdf.
2. Ibid.
3. Ibid.
4. See e.g., U.S. Dep't of Army, Field Manual 3-24, Counterinsurgency (Dec. 15, 2006).
5. U.S. Dep't of Army, Reg. 27-20, Claims (Feb. 8, 2008), para. 10-3(a).
6. See Multi-National Corps – Iraq, Commander's Emergency Response Program (CERP) Family of Fund Standard Operating Procedures, April 24, 2006.
7. See General Accountability Office, The Department of Defense's Use of Solatia and Condolence Payments in Iraq and Afghanistan, May 2007; Tina Susman, "A Martyr and More in his Mother's Eyes," Los Angeles Times, Mar. 6, 2008; Sharon Behn, "U.S. Paid $42.4 Million to Iraqis," Washington Times, Feb. 28, 2008; Special Inspector General for Iraq Reconstruction, Quarterly Report to Congress, Jan. 30, 2008.
8. See http://www.aclu.org/natsec/foia/search.html.
193. See http://www.aclu.org/natsec/foia/pdf/Army1161_1164.pdf.
194. See http://www.aclu.org/natsec/foia/pdf/Army0686_0689.pdf.
195. See http://www.aclu.org/natsec/foia/pdf/Army0478_0482.pdf.
196. Ibid.

197. Ibid.
199. See http://www.aclu.org/natsec/foia/pdf/Army1380_1384.pdf.
200. Ibid.
201. See http://www.aclu.org/natsec/foia/pdf/Army0439_0454.pdf.
202. See http://www.aclu.org/natsec/foia/pdf/Army0439_0454.pdf.
203. Ibid.
204. Ibid.

In Iraq, Study Shows Military, Moral, and Legal Value in Minimizing Civilian Casualties

Andrew Shaver and Jacob N. Shapiro

In the following excerpted viewpoint authors Andrew Shaver and Jacob N. Shapiro argue that the information given on rebels by nonmilitary personnel has been useful for the governments involved. In their study of Iraqi civilian abuse between June 2007–July 2008, the authors determine a correlation between civilian casualties and information flow. They surmise that the US military policy to minimize these casualties is well placed, based on findings indicating civilian casualties caused by the US-led coalition led to increases in Iraqi violence. Shaver and Shapiro were affiliated with Princeton University's Woodrow Wilson School of Public & International Affairs when this article was first published.

As you read, consider the following questions:

1. What is the relationship between wartime information flow and civilian protection?
2. How do "tips" from civilians affect the cost of war?
3. What is the value of using both quantitative and qualitative data?

"The Effect of Civilian Casualties on Wartime Informing: Evidence from the Iraq War," by Andrew Shaver and Jacob N. Shapiro, Trustees of Princeton University, January 3, 2016. Reprinted by permission.

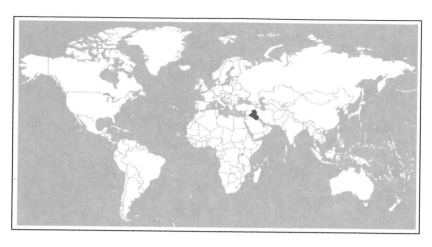

Civilians often bear significant costs of fighting between parties to sub-state conflicts. In Afghanistan, an estimated 21,000 civilians have "died violent deaths as a result of the [ongoing] war" (Costs of War Project, 2014). In Iraq, between 134,789 and 152,104 civilians have been killed since the United States invasion in 2003 (Iraq Body Count, 2008). The toll in Syria has been even greater. Price et al. (2014) calculate that nearly 200,000 individuals have been killed during that country's four-year old civil war.[1] And these numbers do not include the grievous injuries suffered by many of the conflicts' civilian survivors. While some 3,200 civilians are reported to have been killed in fighting between the Taliban and Afghan forces in 2014, more than twice as many Afghans were wounded during the same period (Johnson, 2014).

Scholars have long posited that insurgent organizations and their state enemies incur costs for the collateral damage they cause. Most twentieth-century counterinsurgency theorists writing on the wars of decolonization argued that obtaining information on rebels from non-combatants was critical for government forces and that protecting the population from insurgents was critical to gaining that cooperation (Trinquier 1961; Galula 1964; Taber 1965; Clutterbuck 1966; Thompson 1966; Kitson 1977). More recently, Kalyvas (2006) argued that indiscriminate violence against civilians is counterproductive because it can turn civilians against the party causing them harm.[2] Berman et al. (2011) explicitly model the relationship between harm and informing as part of a 3-sided game in which civilians punish insurgents who create excessive costs by sharing information with government forces.

Indirect empirical support for this relationship has been identified in a number of conflicts. US government officials cited the potential for civilian casualties to harm cooperation from civilians as one reason for imposing more restrictive rules of engagement in Afghanistan in 2009. Condra and Shapiro (2012) show that in Iraq insurgent violence went up after Coalition-caused civilian casualties and down after insurgent-caused ones, consistent with an informational reaction to abuse. Lyall et al. (2013a) show that self-reported victimization by the International Security Assistance Force (ISAF) correlates with lower support for ISAF and higher support for the Taliban. Shapiro and Weidmann (2015) provide evidence that plausibly exogenous increases in cell phone coverages led to lower insurgent violence during the Iraq war, which they attribute to greater information flow to counterinsurgents as the presence of mobile telecommunications lowered the risks of informing.

What is missing in these papers is direct evidence on information flow to counterinsurgents. As one recent paper puts it, "despite its central role in civil war dynamics, the act of informing is still poorly understood, due mostly to the classified nature of informant tips" (Lyall et al., 2013b).

Using newly declassified data on weekly province-level tips collected by Iraqi and Coalition force during the Iraq war, we provide the first direct test of the influence of civilian abuse on wartime informing. Our data span all thirteen provinces which experienced substantial violence over a 60-week period from June 2007 to July 2008. We combine the data on tips with administratively-collected geolocated data on combat violence and press-based data on civilian casualties. We buttress our quantitative analysis with anecdotes from rich qualitative documentation on intelligence collection in Iraq obtained through Freedom of Information Act (FOIA) requests.

Exploiting plausibly exogenous variation in civilian casualties occurring during combat incidents we find a robust relationship between indiscriminate violence and informing. In our baseline model, an additional Coalition-caused civilian casualty leads to approximately .8 fewer tips in the next week, while an additional insurgent-caused one leads to approximately .5 more tips. Consistent with prior work we find that government forces pay a higher cost for causing casualties in so far as the drop in tip flows following a single government-caused casualties is roughly 60% larger than the increase following insurgent caused ones.[3] These effects, while modest in magnitude, are substantively significant. In the median week in which insurgents caused civilian casualties, they killed four civilians, predicting two additional tips to Coalition forces. That is a substantial number (roughly 10% of the weekly mean) since single tips often resulted in raids that led to the capture of both large numbers of weapons and prominent insurgents.

From a scientific standpoint, these results provide the first direct statistical evidence for a relationship scholars and practitioners have posited for more than 50 years. One can interpret our estimates as reflecting a causal effect to the extent that he or she believes the spikes in civilian casualties from week-to-week are conditionally independent of the next week's trend in informing. As we will see, the results below are extremely stable across different specifications, lending credence to that interpretation.

From a policy perspective, our findings reinforce the importance of minimizing collateral damage. In addition to the ethical imperative that combatants take all reasonable measures to avoid harming civilians, they appear to face strategic incentives to do so as well: at least in Iraq members of the public penalized parties who did not.

This paper proceeds as follows: in the following section, we consider the possible effect(s) of civilian casualties on battlefield outcomes and why incidents of collateral damage should be expected to affect wartime informing. We then introduce our data and empirical strategy. Finally, we present results and conclude with a discussion of policy implications.

[...]

Our main contribution is thus to conclusively demonstrate the existence of an informational channel by which combatant behavior can impact conflict outcomes and to do so using data that until now has remained classified and thus unavailable for research. The relationship we observe is not surprising. Many scholars have found indirect evidence of this phenomenon previously. What is unique in this study is that we directly observe information flow and are able to benchmark the magnitude of the difference in non-combatant response to the two sides. Consistent with prior work, we find that government forces pay a higher price for inflicting the same level of harm, though the difference is statistically modest.

From a policy perspective these results clearly indicate that the US military's focus in training and doctrine on avoiding harm to civilians is well placed. As Condra et al. (2010) observe, "in addition to moral and legal concerns, there may be military strategic value in reducing civilian casualties." Our results offer quantitative evidence that this is indeed the case. In contemporary counterinsurgency campaigns marked by the deployment of anonymous tips platforms, both the insurgency and its state challenger pay a price for harming civilians.

Endnotes

1. Though this estimate does not distinguish between civilians and combatants, the Syrian Observatory for Human Rights contends that 62,347 of these individuals were civilians (Alfred, 2014).
2. Though see Lyall (2009) for evidence to the contrary from the Chechen war.
3. The difference is modestly significant statistically, $t=1.48$, $p=.16$, using standard clustered s.e..

Judicial and Nonjudicial Approaches Are Necessary to Prosecute and Prevent Civilian Deaths

Alejandra Vicente

In the following excerpted viewpoint, Alejandra Vicente recommends a two-pronged approach toward prosecuting and preventing civilian deaths to achieve peace in the short term and reconciliation in the long term. These two approaches call for both judicial and nonjudicial methodologies. Vicente outlines the possibilities for each approach and presents case studies of Rwanda and Sierra Leone, evaluating the effectiveness of prosecution in both national courts and international tribunals. She also highlights the addition of truth commissions as a contemporary approach. Vicente is Senior Legal Advisor, Center for Justice and International Law, The Hague, The Netherlands.

As you read, consider the following questions:

1. Which international law bodies work to prosecute perpetrators of civilian deaths?
2. What is another term to describe judicial justice? Nonjudicial justice?
3. What are the criticisms of the Rwandan tribunal?

"Justice Against Perpetrators, The Role of Prosecution in Peacemaking and Reconciliation," by Alejandra Vicente, BADIL Resource Center, April 2003. Reprinted by permission.

I n today's world, issues of peace and international justice are receiving increasing attention. This working paper will examine the relationship between these two concepts—peace and justice— and the impact of prosecution on peacemaking, in the short term, and reconciliation, in the long term.

The importance of prosecuting crimes after a repressive regime or a conflict, and the impact prosecution has on peacemaking and reconciliation, cannot be discussed without making a reference to other approaches aiming reconciliation. In the last century, the international community has passed from accepting amnesty laws as the standard way to secure peace, to consider that punishment before national or international courts is a preferred solution for achieving justice and reconciliation. Meanwhile, a third alternative is emerging with characteristics of both—the truth commission, or truth and reconciliation commission.

With the internationalization of human rights and humanitarian law, the international community has shown its repulsion against human rights abuses, and its preference for prosecuting the perpetrators of crimes over granting them amnesty.[1] This preference for prosecution is reflected in some legal instruments, such as the Genocide Convention of 1948 or the Geneva Conventions of 1949, as well as in international institutions, such as the Inter-American Court and Commission of Human Rights, or the UN Human Rights Committee among others.

However, among scholars, there is a strong debate on the most effective ways to aim peace and reconciliation, suggesting a dichotomy between judicial and non judicial approaches, or what some authors call retributive justice against reconciliatory justice.[2]

This working paper adopts an approach to this debate in the context of contemporary international law. In its first part, an overview of the different judicial and non-judicial approaches to deal with past conflict, as well as an analysis of their effective contribution to peace and reconciliation through several experiences, is presented. In the second part, the author examines the International Criminal Tribunal for the Former Yugoslavia as one of the main judicial approaches currently functioning, and its role in achieving peace and reconciliation in the Balkans.

Towards Reconciliation: Different Approaches and Their Practical Application

In the decades immediately following World War II, advocates for human rights launched three important innovations: International Military Tribunal trials in Nuremberg and Tokyo, the United Nations, and intergovernmental and nongovernmental organizations. More recently, mechanisms for the promotion and protection of human rights include as well ad hoc international tribunals (ICTY and ICTR), truth commissions, and the permanent International Criminal Court among others.

As it is shown throughout this paper, each of these mechanisms has been applied in very different situations and conflicts with different characteristics, but all of them intend to deal with the past and to prevent the recurrence of conflict and serious crimes. Among these approaches, it is possible to make a distinction between non-judicial and judicial mechanisms.

Non Judicial Approaches: Amnesty Laws and Truth Commissions

- Amnesty laws. The traditional approach to the intersection of peace and justice was the amnesty law, by which outgoing authorities granted themselves, or negotiate the granting of, amnesty. Not surprisingly, this mechanism has been abused many times in the past by repressive military or other regimes seeking impunity for their crimes before relinquishing power to successor governments. However, it can be argued that, at certain points in history, amnesty was the only approach to smoothly reach a democratic transition after a repressive regime, and thus may have represented the best available option to victims as well as perpetrators.[3] The recent trend in international law, however, has been to reject amnesty laws. For example, the U.N. Commission on Human Rights and its Sub-Commission for the Prevention of Discrimination and Protection of Minorities have concluded that amnesty is a major reason for continuing human rights violations throughout the world.[4] Also the Inter-American Court and Commission of Human Rights have held that amnesties granted by several Latin American countries are incompatible with the American Convention of Human Rights. However, a compromise between the international demand for prosecution of international crimes and the national appeal for a political compromise involving amnesty can in some cases be achieved by recognizing a distinction between permissible and impermissible amnesties, and by giving international acceptance to the former only.[5]

- Truth and Reconciliation Commissions. In the last decades, and after facing atrocities such as those committed in Chile, South Africa, Uganda and Cambodia, the enforcement of human rights has required the development of creative alternatives. Among the most remarkable is the development of truth commissions intended to inquire and document torture, murders, and other human rights violations that otherwise would be denied and covered up by repressive regimes. This approach constitutes a new form of dealing with the past that could be located between amnesty laws and international or national tribunals, and sometimes is applied together with one of these two mechanisms. As it is shown in the next section, truth commissions have come to constitute an effective way to deal with the past and achieve reconciliation in several experiences, the best known and perhaps most successful in South Africa.

[...]

Judicial approaches for dealing with the past

Judicial approaches to deal with the past are applied in different legal scenarios and with different features, but most of them are characterized by being retributive and, in most of the cases, although not necessarily, adversarial. Among them it is possible to distinguish:

- Military tribunals, such as Nuremberg and Tokyo. These Tribunals were a reaction to the holocaust and other atrocities committed during World War II. Although their relevance from a historical point of view has been remarkable, this approach is widely seen today as victor's justice and therefore not conducive to reconciliation.

- Ad hoc tribunals such as the ones created for Yugoslavia and Rwanda. Following massive violations of human rights, including genocide, which were considered threats to international peace and security, the Security Council, acting under Chapter VII of the U.N. Charter, created the two ad hoc Tribunals as a measure contributing to the restoration and maintenance of peace in those areas.

- National courts applying the principle of universal jurisdiction, such as Belgium with its case against Sharon or Spain with its case against Pinochet. The effect of the case against General Pinochet on Chilean society was considered in the previous section.

- National courts prosecuting the perpetrators in their own jurisdictions and under their own judicial system, such as in Chile or Rwanda. In this latter case, discussed below, national prosecution is complemented by the Rwandan International Criminal Tribunal.

- Special courts created by agreement, such as in Sierra Leone, representing a mixture of national and international law.

- The International Court of Justice and the International Criminal Court in The Hague. Although different in nature and in procedures, both mechanisms constitute international fora in which countries can bring their grievances regarding

Nearly 75 Percent of Iraqi Civilian Deaths Caused by Unknown Perpetrators

Armed violence is a major public health and humanitarian problem in Iraq. In this descriptive statistical analysis we aimed to describe for the first time Iraqi civilian deaths caused by perpetrators of armed violence during the first 5 years of the Iraq war: over time; by weapon used; by region (governorate); and by victim demographics.

We analyzed the Iraq Body Count database of 92,614 Iraqi civilian direct deaths from armed violence occurring from March 20, 2003 through March 19, 2008, of which Unknown perpetrators caused 74% of deaths (n=68,396), Coalition forces 12% (n=11,516), and Anti-Coalition forces 11% (n=9,954). We analyzed the subset of 60,481 civilian deaths from 14,196 short-duration events of lethal violence to link individual civilian deaths to events involving perpetrators and their methods. One-third of civilian violent death was from extrajudicial executions by Unknown perpetrators; quadratic regression shows these deaths progressively and disproportionately increased as deaths from other forms of violence increased across Iraq's governorates. The highest average number of civilians killed per event in which a civilian died were in Unknown perpetrator suicide bombings targeting civilians (19 per lethal event) and Coalition aerial bombings (17 per lethal event). In temporal analysis, numbers of civilian deaths from Coalition air attacks, and woman and child deaths from Coalition forces, peaked during the invasion. We applied a Woman and Child "Dirty War Index" (DWI), measuring the proportion of women and children among civilian deaths of known demographic status, to the 22,066 civilian victims identified as men, women, or children to indicate relatively indiscriminate perpetrator effects. DWI findings suggest the most indiscriminate effects on women and children were from Unknown perpetrators using mortar fire (DWI =79) and nonsuicide vehicle bombs (DWI =54) and from Coalition air attacks (DWI =69). Coalition forces had higher Woman and Child DWIs than Anti-Coalition forces, with no evidence of decrease over 2003–2008, for all weapons combined and for small arms gunfire, specifically.

Most Iraqi civilian violent deaths during 2003–2008 of the Iraq war were inflicted by Unknown perpetrators, primarily through extrajudicial executions that disproportionately increased in regions with greater numbers of violent deaths. Unknown perpetrators using suicide bombs, vehicle bombs, and mortars had highly lethal and indiscriminate effects on the Iraqi civilians they targeted. Deaths caused by Coalition forces of Iraqi civilians, women, and children peaked during the invasion period, with relatively indiscriminate effects from aerial weapons.

"Violent Deaths of Iraqi Civilians, 2003–2008: Analysis by Perpetrator, Weapon, Time, and Location," by Madelyn Hsiao-Rei Hicks, Hamit Dardagan, Gabriela Guerrero Serdan, Peter M. Bagnall, John A. Sloboda, and Michael Spagat, Public Library of Science, 02/15/2011.

human rights violations. In particular, the recently created International Criminal Court represents the future of prosecution for human rights violations.

Two of these many examples—those of Rwanda and Sierra Leone—are discussed below.

Rwanda

The Rwandan conflict represents one of the worst atrocities ever committed, both for its intensity and for its efficiency and calculated organization. The conflict was the result of fighting between the two main ethnic groups, Hutus and Tutsis, over political power and access to resources and wealth. As Vandeginste notes "[d]ealing with the past in such a context cannot solely be a judicial issue; it is a political challenge and a challenge for society as a whole."[17] He also recognizes that Rwanda has not yet reached a political transition process aimed at representation, inclusiveness and better governance. Although the Arusha Accords included power sharing and numerical distribution of seats in the transitional National Assembly, this agreement has not been implemented.

In this context, two different approaches to dealing with the Rwandan conflict have arisen: an ad hoc tribunal created by the international community, and a reformed national judicial system.

On one hand, due to the reaction of the international community to the atrocities committed in Rwanda between April and June 1994, the International Criminal Tribunal for Rwanda was created by U.N Security Council Resolution 955 of 8 November 1994. The Tribunal's Statute recognizes that the role of the Tribunal is to "contribute to the process of national reconciliation and to the restoration and maintenance of peace."[18]

However, despite the high expectations of the Rwandan population, the Rwanda Tribunal has been criticized for various reasons. Among them, it is worth noting the delay in its procedures, its temporal limit (as the Tribunal's mandate only covers crimes committed in 1994), lack of investigation on the crimes committed by the victor (Tutsis), and lack of involvement of victims in the process.

On the other hand, the response of the national judicial system was the consequence of the new government's will to prosecute the perpetrators of mass human rights violations as a precondition for reconciliation in the country. To that aim, two objectives were essential and consecutive: the re-establishment of the justice system, and the prosecution of genocide crimes within that system.

In spite of its achievements, some problems remain with the national justice system as well, such as the delay and quality of the proceedings (which do not always follow recognized international standards), the fact that the justice system is seen by the Hutus as the victor's justice system, and the lack of victim's participation in the process. Some of the justifications given to these obstacles are the magnitude of the conflict and the limit in the capacity of the judicial system and economic situation of the country to deal with individual criminal trials.

In Rwanda, therefore, prosecution seems to have been insufficient to bring reconciliation. As Vandegiste notes, "[f]or justice to be accepted as an instrument of reconciliation, it must meet certain conditions that go even beyond criteria of the independence and impartiality of the judiciary. These conditions include its embeddedness in an overall process toward transparency, political participation, and inclusiveness."[19]

Sierra Leone

In response to atrocities committed in the country as a consequence of a civil war in the 1990s, the Security Council, by its resolution 1315 (2000) of 14 August 2000, requested the Secretary General of the United Nations to negotiate an agreement with the Government of Sierra Leone to create an independent special court to prosecute persons who bear the greatest responsibility for the commission of crimes against humanity, war crimes and other serious violations of international humanitarian law committed within the territory of Sierra Leone.[20] It is important to note that, unlike the Yugoslavia Tribunal, which was created under Chapter VII of the U.N. Charter, the Special Court was the result of an agreement signed between the United Nations and the Sierra Leonean Government on 16 January 2002. As a consequence, the Special Court has concurrent jurisdiction with primacy only over Sierra Leonean courts.

The subject matter jurisdiction of the Court includes crimes under international law (crimes against humanity, war crimes and other serious violations of international humanitarian law not including the crime of genocide), and crimes under Sierra Leonean law.[21]

Although the civil war started in 1991, the temporal jurisdiction of the Court is since 30 September 1996 when the first peace agreement between the parts collapsed and the hostilities resumed with great violence. As its negotiators noted, temporal jurisdiction since the beginning of hostilities in 1991 would have been too ambitious a project, considering the economic and temporal constraints, and may have endangered the viability and success of the Court.

The Statute of the Court specifically provides that an amnesty granted to any person falling within the jurisdiction of the Special Court, in respect of the crimes referred to in the Statute, shall not be bar to prosecution. The Special Court thus recognizes the prevailing rejection of amnesty under international law and avoids any kind of impunity for the perpetrators.

The Special Court of Sierra Leone is innovative in several respects, relative to the Rwanda and Yugoslavia Tribunals. In addition to the incorporation of national law, several judges and staff members are from the country or appointed by its Government, and the seat of the Tribunal is in the country's capital, Freetown.

Since most of the Court's judges were sworn in during December 2002, is still very early to evaluate the role that this judicial mechanism will have in achieving lasting peace and reconciliation in Sierra Leone.

[...]

Endnotes

1. See Mary Margaret Penrose, "It's Good to Be the King!: Prosecuting Heads of State and Former Heads of State under International Law," Columbia Journal of Transnational Law, 2000, at 193-220. In her article, Professor Penrose advocates the enactment of prosecutorial rules and urges the international community and states in particular to take the necessary steps to try the perpetrators. See also David Scheffer's (U.S. Ambassador for War Crimes Issues) Address at Dartmourth College, 23 October 1998, in which the author notes "[A] s the most powerful nation committed to the rule of law, we have a responsibility to confront these assaults on humankind. One response mechanism is accountability, namely to help bring the perpetrators of genocide, crimes against humanity, and war crimes to justice. If we allow them to act with impunity, then we will only be inviting a perpetuation of these crimes far into the next millennium. Our legacy must demonstrate an unyielding commitment to the pursuit of justice."

2. See John Dugard, "Dealing with Crimes of a Past Regime. Is Amnesty Still an Option?" 12 Leiden Journal of International Law, at 1005. See also Tuomas Forsberg, "The Philosophy and Practice of Dealing with the Past: Some Conceptual and Normative Issues," at 62, in Nigel Biggar, Burying the Past. Making Peace and doing Justice after Civil Conflict. Washington, DC: Georgetown University Press, 2001.

3. Note for instance, the post-Franco Spain or the post-Pinochet Chile.

4. See, United Nations Commission on Human Rights: Report on the Consequences of Impunity, U.N. Doc. E/.CN.4/ 1990/13.

5. See the comparison between the experiences of Chile and South Africa noted by John Dugard, supra note 2 "Dealing with Crimes of a Past Regime. Is Amnesty Still an Option?" at 1001-1015.

17. See Stef Vandeginste, "Rwanda: Dealing with Genocide and Crimes against Humanity in the Context of Armed Conflict and Failed Political Transition," at 223, in Biggar, supra note 3.

18. In this sense is important to mention Prosecutor v. Serusago, Sentence, Case No. ICTR-98-39-S, T. Ch I, 5 February 1999, para. 19; Prosecutor v. Kambanda, Judgment and Sentence, Case No. ICTR-97-23-S, T Ch. I, 4 September 1998, paras. 26-28 (see also para. 59); Prosecutor v. Rutaganda, Judgement and Sentence, Case No. ICTR-96-3-T, T. Ch. I, 6 December 1999, paras. 455-456.

19. See above Vandeginste, supra note 17, at 246.

20. See Report of the Secretary-General on the establishment of a Special Court for Sierra Leone, 4 October 2000, (S/2000/915).
21. One notable innovation of the Court is its personal jurisdiction over juvenile offenders who, at the time of the alleged commission of the crime, were between 15 and 18 years of age. See Article 7 of the Statute of the Special Court, regarding "Jurisdiction over persons of 15 years of age." This point was highly controversial at the time of the negotiations and, due to the pressure from different human rights organizations, measures of rehabilitation and other judicial guarantees were contemplated.

In Vietnam, Many Factors Led US Soldiers to Massacre Civilians in My Lai

George Herring

In the following viewpoint, George Herring argues that although US engagement in Vietnam began in the 1950s to contain Communism, by 1968, the fighting had morphed into a full-fledged battle without a front. With a measure of success that valued body count, the soldiers of the first platoon of Charlie Company, led by Lieutenant William Calley, attacked the village of My Lai. The author evaluates the factors that led to this massacre, the charge of murder levied against Calley, and the outcome of his trial. Herring is an alumni professor of history at the University of Kentucky.

As you read, consider the following questions:

1. How did Americans view the My Lai incident?
2. What factors incited the soldiers of Calley's platoon to kill Vietnamese civilians?
3. What was the outcome of the trial against Calley?

The United States' involvement in Vietnam expanded through a series of stages between 1950 and 1965. From 1950 to 1954, in the name of containing communism, the US assisted the French in fighting a Communist-led nationalist revolution

"The Vietnam War and the My Lai Massacre," by George Herring, The Gilder Lehrman Institute of American History. Reprinted by permission.

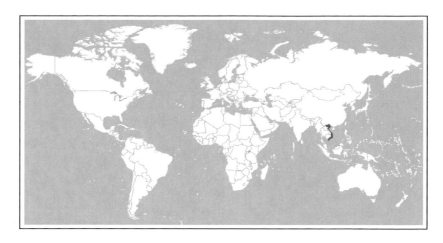

in Vietnam, ultimately paying close to 80 percent of the cost of the war. From 1954 to 1961, after the French had departed, the American government attempted to construct in the southern part of Vietnam an independent, non-Communist nation to stand as a bulwark against further Communist expansion in Southeast Asia. From 1961 to 1965, the United States assisted the South Vietnamese in fighting an internal insurgency backed by Communist North Vietnam. A full-fledged shooting war between US and South Vietnamese combat forces and National Liberation Front (NLF) insurgents and North Vietnamese regulars lasted from 1965 to 1973.

After 1965, the United States undertook what one top official with no apparent sense of paradox described as an "all-out limited war" in Vietnam. US aircraft carried out bombing campaigns in South and North Vietnam that in time exceeded the tonnage dropped by all nations in all theaters in World War II. By 1968, the United States had more than 500,000 troops in South Vietnam fighting a variety of wars in different regions. Along the demilitarized zone separating North from South Vietnam, US Marines and North Vietnamese regulars were dug in like the armies of World War I pounding each other with artillery. In other parts of South Vietnam, major increments of US forces conducted massive "search-and-destroy" operations to root out NLF and

North Vietnamese regulars. In remote areas, small units probed inhospitable terrain in search of an elusive but deadly enemy. In villages across South Vietnam, military personnel and civilians conducted "pacification" operations designed, in the phrase of the day, to win the hearts and minds of the people. Even with this level of engagement, the best the United States could achieve was a costly stalemate. The massive North Vietnamese-NLF Tet Offensive of February 1968 escalated the violence still further. For the first time, the enemy struck with lethal force at the major towns and cities of South Vietnam, even the supposedly secure capital of Saigon, sparking heavy fighting nationwide. The United States and South Vietnam regained what been lost, but at enormous cost and with huge destruction and loss of life.

The My Lai massacre occurred in the immediate aftermath of the Tet Offensive. On March 16, 1968, the soldiers of Charlie Company, First Battalion, Americal Division, helicoptered into what they called My Lai 4, a hamlet in the larger village of Son My in Quang Ngai province, a beautiful but for Americans deadly region along the northeastern coast of South Vietnam and for years an enemy stronghold. Charlie Company was part of Task Force Barker, commanded by LTC Frank Barker and given the mission to root out NLF units deeply entrenched in the area. CPT Ernest Medina headed Charlie Company; 2nd LT William Calley commanded the First Platoon. Bravo Company undertook a similar operation in nearby My Khe.

The savagery that followed defies description. Geared up for action, the men entered My Lai at 8 a.m. with weapons blazing and for the next four hours engaged in an orgy of killing. "We just rounded 'em up, me and a couple of guys, just put the M-16 on automatic, & just mowed 'em down," one soldier later recalled. Meeting no resistance, the Americans killed old men, women, and even children and babies. They burned homes and destroyed livestock. There were rapes. The GIs suffered but one casualty, a self-inflicted wound to a single soldier. The company's after-action report counted 128 "enemy" dead and—tellingly—three weapons captured. An official account boasted that Task Force Barker had "crushed an enemy stronghold." The carnage might have been worse without the courageous intervention of helicopter pilot Hugh Thompson, decorated many years later, who, upon witnessing the scene from above landed and protected a small group of Vietnamese by threatening his fellow soldiers with his machine guns.

Among a people that have historically prided themselves on their exceptional virtue, the question that still lingers is how could My Lai happen. Part of the answer rests with the way the war in Vietnam was fought. All wars produce atrocities. Since World War II, moreover, civilians have increasingly been victimized. In Vietnam, the United States relied on its technological superiority, mainly its massive firepower, to disrupt enemy operations, kill enemy soldiers, and inflict sufficient pain on the NLF and North Vietnam that they would be persuaded to cease the fight. In a war without front lines, the principal measure of progress was the notorious body count, which incited GIs to kill as many enemy as possible. In a guerrilla war like Vietnam, the distinction between warrior and civilian was often blurred. Many villages willingly or under duress harbored guerrilla fighters. To the GIs, civilians were often indistinguishable from guerrillas and thought to be in league with them.

The mentality of war also contributed to My Lai. The soldiers of Charlie Company brought to this operation a melange of intense emotions: fear, anger, a lust for revenge, even a sort of emotional numbness that deadened normal human inhibitions. One of the company's troopers had been killed by a sniper on February 12, its first death in Vietnam. In the weeks that followed, others were killed or wounded by booby traps and land mines, even though the company had never actually seen, much less engaged the enemy. These conditions provoked in the Americans anger, frustration, and a determination to avenge their buddies, manifesting itself even before My Lai in the increasingly brutal treatment of Vietnamese civilians, including several reported rapes. The day before the action, the company held a highly emotional memorial service for a fallen comrade. The formal briefing for My Lai followed soon after and further conditioned the men for revenge. The soldiers thus vented their rage on civilians who were deemed to be the enemy or at least in league with the enemy.

Leaders from the top down failed abjectly in planning, preparation, and execution of the operation. Senior officers ordered an attack they believed would demonstrate to the people of Quang Ngai the costs of harboring the enemy. The plan was based on faulty assumptions regarding enemy strength and the presence of civilians. The soldiers were told that the area was full of NLF sympathizers and must be cleaned out. Civilians would be at market. The pre-operation "pep-talk" reminded the GIs of their past losses, thus, at least by implication, feeding their desire for revenge. It said nothing about dealing with civilians. Leaders on the ground failed to lead. Calley was young, inexperienced, and by most accounts incompetent. Officers and non-coms got caught up in a herd mentality. Senior officers such as Barker and Medina had some idea what was going on but failed to intervene.

These same officers participated in a full-fledged cover-up. No one bothered to question the apparent discrepancies in the after-action report. Those who knew the truth sat on it or looked the other way. An order to go back to My Lai and take a second look was countermanded by MG Samuel Koster. In violation of Army regulations, the division command allowed the brigade to do its own investigation. CL Oran Henderson, the brigade commander, conducted a perfunctory investigation, admitting only that twenty "non-combatants" had been killed accidentally. Thompson's superiors did not follow up on his reports. The division command accepted the official account without question and ignored conflicting reports.

The horrific story of My Lai was finally revealed more than eighteen months later by an intrepid and conscience-stricken former GI, Ron Ridenhour, who initially heard about it in a bar and traced various leads to get the facts. Ridenhour's letter to a

Congressional committee prompted an Army investigation that led to charges against Calley in September 1969. The story of Calley's indictment in turn spurred investigative reporter Seymour Hersh to uncover the truth, which he published in November. Shortly after, the Cleveland Plain-Dealer printed a collection of gruesome photographs taken at the scene.

The nation's reaction to My Lai mirrored its attitudes toward a war that by November 1969 had become markedly unpopular. The press properly expressed horror at the revelations, but it also treated My Lai ethnocentrically as an American story. Some blamed the war itself rather than the men of Charlie Company. Many newspapers that opposed the war saw in My Lai added reason to end it as soon as possible. Some also questioned why it took so long for the story to come out. The public judged My Lai similarly. Some of those who still backed the war questioned whether My Lai had happened at all or blamed the media for publicizing it. Others pointed out that the enemy committed atrocities as a matter of policy. Those who wanted the war to end were appalled at the horror and pressed for its termination.

Under the glare of media publicity and public discussion, the Army sought to deal with My Lai through its legal system. Thirteen soldiers were charged with murder. The charges against six were dropped for lack of evidence; six were tried in military courts and found not guilty. Twelve officers were accused of a cover-up. Only Henderson went to trial. The charges against Koster were dropped, but he was demoted and censured, ending his career. The trial of Calley for murder drew as much attention as the incident itself. In March 1971, he was found guilty of murder and sentenced to life imprisonment at hard labor. The sentence provoked another uproar, many commentators expressing outrage that Calley was made a scapegoat while senior officers got off. President Richard M. Nixon intervened by agreeing to review the case, setting off more outrage. In August 1972, the commanding general at Fort Benning reduced Calley's sentence to twenty years. Two years later, a US District Court freed him on bail and made him eligible for parole in six months. Later that year, another federal court overturned his conviction on grounds that the pre-trial publicity had made a fair trial impossible.

In Vietnam and the United States, memories of My Lai have dimmed over the years. Americans, including some veterans, helped construct a hospital at the site of the massacre and a "peace park" to remind future generations of the horrors of war. For those Vietnamese who lost loved ones, of course, forgetting is impossible. Yet even in Vietnam there are signs of a desire to move on. Luxury beachfront hotels have been constructed near My Khe as part of the nation's campaign to attract tourists. In the United States, the Army has determinedly attempted to use My Lai to train officers and men in problems of military ethics and leadership. Yet atrocities continue, whether the mistreatment of prisoners at Abu Ghraib prison in Iraq, the massacre of unarmed Iraqis by US Marines at the side of a roadside bombing in Hidatha, Iraq, or in the indiscriminate killing of civilians, often by high technology weapons, in Afghanistan. And for most Americans, My Lai is forgotten. Inasmuch as they recall Vietnam, they see themselves as victims and evince little sympathy for the Vietnamese. If the United States is to live up to the high ideals it professes to believe in, events such as My Lai must be remembered and must be seen not simply in terms of the impact upon ourselves but also on the horrors visited on others. The courageous efforts of heroes like Hugh Thompson and Ron Ridenour offer compelling examples of what individuals can do to stop or expose injustice.

Periodical and Internet Sources Bibliography

The following articles have been selected to supplement the diverse views presented in this chapter.

Amnesty International, "Afghanistan: Left in the Dark: Failure of Accountability for Civilian Casualties Caused by International Military Operations," August 11, 2014. https://www.amnesty.nl/content/uploads/2016/11/amnesty_afghanistan_final_report.pdf?x54649.

Amnesty International, "Afghanistan: No Justice for Thousands of Civilians Killed in US/NATO Operations," August 11, 2014. https://www.amnesty.org/en/latest/news/2014/08/afghanistan-no-justice-thousands-civilians-killed-usnato-operations/.

Bruce Cronin, "Reckless Endangerment Warfare: Civilian Casualties and the Collateral Damage Exception in International Humanitarian Law," *Journal of Peace Research*, March 2013.

Akmal Dawi, "Cash and Heaven: How Afghan War Victims Are Compensated," Voice of America, August 28, 2014. https://www.voanews.com/a/afghanistan-war-collateral-casualty-compensation-karzai-nato-us-taliban/2431009.html.

Amitai Etzioni, "Who Causes Civilian Casualties?" *Army*, November 2015.

Seymour M. Hersh, "The Scene of the Crime," *New Yorker*, March 30, 2015.

Sarah Holewinski, "Do Less Harm: Protecting and Compensating Civilians in War," *Foreign Affairs*, January/February 2013.

Joshua Kelly, "Re Civilian Casualty Court Martial: Prosecuting Breaches of International Humanitarian Law Using the Australian Military Justice System," *Melbourne University Law Review*, 2013. http://law.unimelb.edu.au/__data/assets/pdf_file/0010/1699021/37_2_3.pdf.

Matthew Coen Leep, "Accounting for Their Dead: Responsiveness to Iraqi Civilian Casualties in the US House of Representatives," *International Politics*, January 2015.

Frédéric Mégret, "Beyond 'Gravity': For a Politics of International Criminal Prosecutions," Proceedings of the Annual Meeting (American Society of International Law), vol. 107, International Law in a Multipolar World, 2013.

James Somper, "British Soldiers Cleared of Iraqi Civilian's Death Could Now Face Prosecution," *Independent*, September 18, 2016. http://www.independent.co.uk/news/world/middle-east/british-soldiers-cleared-of-iraqi-civilians-death-could-now-face-prosecution-a7314616.html.

United Nations Mechanism for International Criminal Tribunals, "Legacy Website of the International Criminal Tribunal for Rwanda." http://unictr.unmict.org/.

GLOBALVIEWPOINTS

CHAPTER 3

Civilian Casualties and War Mongering

"New Wars" Wreak Havoc on Civilian Populations

Mary Kaldor

In the following excerpted viewpoint, Mary Kaldor argues that globalization has changed the nature of warfare to what she terms "new wars." She maintains that wars are no longer only fought by a nation's armies. Rather, combatants can include mercenaries, privately contracted forces, and other groups. She also claims that today's wars are fought for ethnic, religious, or tribal identity versus ideology or turf. But it is in the method of these new wars where civilians are at greater risk, because the wars have no specific battlefields. Kaldor is Professor of Global Governance at the London School of Economics.

As you read, consider the following questions:

1. How do "new wars" differ from "old wars" with respect to their methods?
2. Can the features of new wars be found in wars before the twenty-first century?
3. What is the relationship between organized violence and the concept of new wars?

Kaldor, M., (2013). "In Defence of New Wars." Stability: International Journal of Security and Development. 2(1), p.Art. 4. DOI: http://doi.org/10.5334/sta.at

Global systems of the 20th century were designed to address inter-state tensions and civil wars. War between nation-states and civil war have a given logic...21st century violence does not fit the 20th century mould...Violence and conflict have not been banished...But because of the success in reducing inter-state war, the remaining forms of violence do not fit neatly either into "war" or "peace," or into "political" or "criminal" violence.

—World Bank 2011

The idea that twenty-first century organised violence is different from the wars of the twentieth century has been widely debated in both the scholarly and the policy literature. Various terms have been used to conceptualise contemporary conflict—wars among the people, wars of the third kind, hybrid wars, privatized wars, post-modern wars as well as "new wars" (Duffield 2001; Eppler 2002; Hables Gray 1997; Hoffman 2007; Holsti 1996; Kaldor 2012; Munkler 2005; Smith 2005; Snow 1996; Van Creveld 1991). But it is the term "new" that seems to have stuck and become the main butt of the critics.

This article defends the concept of "new wars." Engaging with and countering the various criticisms that have been brought forward against the term "new," it makes the argument that the "new" in "new wars" has to be understood as a research strategy and a guide for policy. Because the "old" is enshrined in the concept of the "new" the term enables us to grapple with the overall logic that is inherent in contemporary violent conflicts and that makes them different in kind from "old wars." It is a logic that goes beyond specific components of contemporary conflicts—identity politics or economic predation, for example. Rather, it provides an integrative framework for analysis.

This essay addresses four main thrusts of criticism: whether new wars are "new"; whether new wars are "war"; whether existing data confirms or negates the findings about the nature of new wars; and whether new wars can be described as post-Clausewitzean. Before doing so, it is worth issuing a note of caution. One of the problems with many of the critics is that they lump together the different versions of the argument and treat criticism of one particular aspect contained in one particular version as a criticism of the whole argument. Such claims include the identification of new wars with civil wars, the claim that they are only fought by non-state actors and only motivated by economic gain, or that they are deadlier than earlier wars (Berdal 2003; de Graaf 2003; Kalyvas 2001; Mellow 2010). In particular, many of the critics employ reductionist arguments whereby new wars are associated with a particular aspect of contemporary wars, for example, crime or privatisation or brutality, and fail to take into account the overall conceptual framework that relates actors, goals, methods and forms of finance. This essay will try to avoid this trap and focus on my own version of New Wars (Kaldor 1999). Before discussing the critiques, I will start with a summary of this particular "new wars" argument.

The Logic of New Wars

New Wars are the wars of the era of globalisation. Typically, they take place in areas where authoritarian states have been greatly weakened as a consequence of opening up to the rest of the world. In such contexts, the distinction between state and non-state, public and private, external and internal, economic and political, and even war and peace are breaking down. Moreover the break down of these binary distinctions is both a cause and a consequence of violence.

New wars have a logic that is different from the logic of what I call "old wars"—the idea of war that predominated in the nineteenth and twentieth centuries. In the original version of the argument, I derived this logic from the differences between old and new wars in actors, goals, methods and forms of finance. These are:

Actors

Old wars were fought by the regular armed forces of states. New wars are fought by varying combinations of networks of state and non-state actors—regular armed forces, private security contractors, mercenaries, jihadists, warlords, paramilitaries, etc.

Goals

Old wars were fought for geo-political interests or for ideology (democracy or socialism). New wars are fought in the name of identity (ethnic, religious or tribal). Identity politics has a different logic from geo-politics or ideology. The aim is to gain access to the state for particular groups (that may be both local and transnational) rather than to carry out particular policies or programmes in the broader public interest. The rise of identity politics is associated with new communications technologies, with migration both from country to town and across the world, and the erosion of more inclusive (often state-based) political ideologies like socialism or post-colonial nationalism. Perhaps most importantly, identity politics is constructed through war. Thus political mobilisation around identity is the aim of war rather than an instrument of war, as was the case in "old wars."

Methods

In old wars, battle was the decisive encounter. The method of waging war consisted of capturing territory through military means. In new wars, battles are rare and territory is captured through political means, through control of the population. A typical technique is population displacement—the forcible removal of those with a different identity or different opinions. Violence is largely directed against civilians as a way of controlling territory rather than against enemy forces.

Forms of Finance

Old wars were largely financed by states (taxation or by outside patrons). In weak states, tax revenue is falling and new forms of predatory private finance include loot and pillage, "taxation" of humanitarian aid, Diaspora support, kidnapping, or smuggling in oil, diamonds, drugs, people, etc. It is sometimes argued that new wars are motivated by economic gain, but it is difficult to distinguish between those who use the cover of political violence for economic reasons and those who engage in predatory economic activities to finance their political cause. Whereas old war economies were typically centralising, autarchic and mobilised the population, new wars are part of an open globalised decentralised economy in which participation is low and revenue depends on continued violence.

The implication of these differences is that, whereas old wars tended to extremes as each side tried to win, new wars tend to spread and to persist or recur as each side gains in political or economic ways from violence itself rather than "winning" (see Keen 2012). Whereas old wars were associated with state building, new wars are the opposite; they tend to contribute to the dismantling of the state.

It is this logic of persistence and spread that I have come to understand as the key difference with old wars—something I elaborate in the last section, where I discuss whether new wars are post-Clausewitzean. Clausewitz was par excellence the theorist of old wars—for him, war was a contest of wills. In my version of new wars, war is rather a violent enterprise framed in political terms. It is important to stress that both old and new wars, in my formulation, are ideal types. They are ideas of war rather than empirical descriptions of war. The test of how well they fit empirical reality depends on whether they provide a guide to useful policy. As I discuss in the following sections, it is this point that is most often missed by the critics of the new wars thesis.

Are New Wars 'New'?

The most common criticism of the "new wars" argument is that new wars are not new. It is argued that the Cold War clouded our ability to analyse "small wars" or "low-intensity wars," that many of the characteristics of new wars associated with weak states can be found in the early modern period and that phenomena like banditry, mass rape, forced population displacement, or atrocities against civilians all have a long history.

Of course this is true. Many of the features of new wars can be found in earlier wars. Of course the dominance of the East-West conflict obscured other types of conflict. But there is an important reason, which is neglected by the preoccupation with empirical claims, for insisting on the adjective "new."

Critics of the "new wars" thesis often concede that what is useful about the analysis of "new wars" is the policy implication of the argument. But this is precisely the point. The term "new" is a way to exclude "old" assumptions about the nature of war and to provide the basis for a novel research methodology. The aim of describing the conflicts of the 1990s as "new" is to change the way scholars investigate these conflicts and thus to change the way policy-makers and policy-shapers perceive these conflicts. Dominant understandings of these conflicts that underpin policy are of two kinds. On the one hand, there is a tendency to impose a stereotyped version of war, drawn from the experience of the last two centuries in Europe, in which war consists of a conflict between two warring parties, generally states or proto-states with legitimate interests, what I call "Old Wars." This term refers to a stylised form of war rather than to all earlier wars. In such wars, the solution is either negotiation or victory by one side and outside intervention takes the form of either traditional peace-keeping—in which the peace-keepers are supposed to guarantee a negotiated agreement and the ruling principles are consent, neutrality and impartiality—or traditional war-fighting on one side or the other, as in Korea or the Gulf War. On the other hand, where policy-makers recognise the shortcomings of the stereotypical understanding, there is a tendency to treat these wars as anarchy, barbarism, ancient rivalries, where the best policy response is containment, i.e. protecting the borders of the West from this malady. The use of the term "new" is a way of demonstrating that neither of these approaches are appropriate, that these are wars with their own logic but a logic that is different from "old wars" and which therefore dictates a very different research strategy and a different policy response. In other words, the "new wars" thesis is both about the changing character of organised violence and about developing a way of understanding, interpreting and explaining the interrelated characteristics of such violence.

[...]

New wars can be described as mixtures of war (organised violence for political ends), crime (organised violence for private ends) and human rights violations (violence against civilians). The advantage of not using the term "war" is that all forms of contemporary violence can be regarded as wholly illegitimate, requiring a policing rather than a political/military response. Moreover, much contemporary violence—like the drugs wars in Mexico or gang warfare in major cities—appears to have a similar logic to new wars, but has to be classified as criminal. The same sort of argument has been used in relation to terrorism. There has been widespread criticism of the term "war on terror" because it implies a military response to terrorist violence when policing and intelligence methods, it is argued, would be more effective (Howard 2002).

On the other hand, the political element does have to be taken seriously; it is part of the solution. Articulating a cosmopolitan politics as an alternative to exclusivist identity is the only way to establish legitimate institutions that can provide the kind of effective governance and security that Mueller is proposing as a solution. War does imply organised violence in the service of political ends. This is the way it legitimises criminal activity. Suicide bombers in their farewell videos describe themselves as soldiers not as murderers. Even if it is the case, and it often is, that those who frame the violence in ethnic, religious or ideological terms are purely instrumental, these political narratives are internalised through the process of engaging in or suffering from violence. Indeed, this is the point of the violence; it is only possible to win elections or to mobilise political support through the politics of fear. This is a point made strongly by Kalyvas in his *Logic of Violence in Civil Wars*. He quotes Thucydides on "the violent fanaticism which came into play once the struggle had broken out ....society had become divided into two ideologically hostile camps, and each side viewed the other with suspicion" (Kalyvas 2006: 78). Overcoming fear and hostility does not necessarily come about through compromise, even if that is possible, because compromise can entrench exclusivist positions; rather it requires a different kind of politics, the construction of a shared discourse that has to underpin any legal response.

[...]

References

Berdal, M 2003 How 'new' are 'new wars'? Global economic change and the study of civil war. Global Governance: 477–502.

De Graaff, B 2003 The wars in former Yugoslavia in the 1990s: Bringing the state back in. In: Angstrom, J and Duyvesteyn, I The Nature of Modern War: Clausewitz and his Critics Revisited. Stockholm: Department of War Studies, Swedish National Defence College.

Duffield, M 2001 Global governance and the new wars: The merging of development and security. London: Zed Books

Eppler, F 2002 Vom Gewaktmärkte zum Gewaltmarkt? Frankfurt: Suhrkmamp.

Hables Gray, C 1997 Post-modern war: The new politics of conflict. London: Routledge.

Hoffman, F 2007 Conflict in the 21st century; The rise of hybrid wars. Arlington: Potomac Institute for Policy Studies.

Holsti, K J 1996 The state, war and the state of war. Cambridge: Cambridge University Press.

Howard, M 2002 What's in a name? Foreign Affairs, January/February 2002.

Kalyvas, S N 2001 'New' and 'old' civil wars: A valid distinction? World Politics 54, October: 99–118.

Kalyvas, S N 2006 The logic of violence in civil wars. Cambridge: Cambridge University Press.

Kaldor, M 1999 New and old wars: Organised violence in a global era. 1st edition. Cambridge: Polity Press.

Mellow, P A 2010 Review article: In search of new wars: The debate about the transformation of war. European Journal of International Relations, 16: 297. DOI: http://dx.doi.org/10.1177/1354066109350053.

Munkler, H 2005 The new wars. Cambridge: Polity Press.

Smith, R 2005 The Utility of Force. London: Alfred A. Knopf.

Snow, D 1996 Uncivil wars: International security and the new internal conflicts. Boulder: Lynne Rienner.

Van Creveld, M 1991 The transformation of war. New York: The Free Press.

World Bank 2011 World Development Report 2011: Conflict, Security and development. Available at http://go.worldbank.org/UCTHLNS530 [Last accessed 5 February 2013].

The Existence of Civilian Casualties Neither Justifies nor Condemns War

Jerome Slater

In the following viewpoint, Jerome Slater argues that the existence of civilian casualties does not mean war is not justified. He further claims that asking the surviving families whether war is justified has no purpose. The issue of civilian casualties raises a number of questions that must be considered before making moral judgments about war. The author maintains World War II was justified despite the civilian casualties, because it stopped Nazi tyranny that might have caused even more deaths than it did. Slater is professor emeritus of international politics, US foreign policy, and international security at the State University of New York at Buffalo.

As you read, consider the following questions:

1. What is American exceptionalism?
2. Is there a certain number of civilian casualties that justifies war?
3. Do all wars cause civilian casualties?

B ecause David Samel raises important issues, and has done so in a courteous but forthright manner, I will try to answer his queries and criticisms, in the same spirit. I have nothing further

"Just wars—and civilian casualties," by Jerome Slater, Mondoweiss, January 9, 2012. Reprinted by permission.

to add to the Ron Paul issue—I think by now everyone's position on the matter is quite clear—so I will focus on the broader issues: noninterventionism, war and peace, civilian casualties, American exceptionalism, and the like.

Samel begins by asking: "Is it really fair to characterize anyone who opposed US military action in Afghanistan, the first Gulf War, Bosnia and Kosovo, Libya etc. as 'simpleminded'?" As Phil Weiss has acknowledged, he wrote the headline on my original post, not me, though it is also true that I did say that "Ron Paul is a simpleminded fool on 90% (at least) of the issues, domestic and foreign." So let me clarify my argument, making the necessary distinctions:

First, I believe that most of Ron Paul's domestic positions are indeed simpleminded, and much worse, disastrous on both moral and consequential grounds. That makes him a fool.

Second, he's not as bad on foreign policy, but bad enough. I would not characterize anyone's opposition to the post-9/11 military action in Afghanistan, the first Gulf War, Bosnia and Kosovo, and Libya as necessarily "simpleminded," though it very well might be, depending on how it is argued. Rather, I say that to the extent such opposition fails to deal with the arguments on both sides, it is, at a minimum, simplistic. For that reason, Ron Paul—but not everyone reaching the same bottom line—is simplistic. Bosnia, Kosovo, and Libya are close calls, with substantial arguments on both sides. However you come out on whether those military interventions were justified, if you don't recognize the complexity of the cases and explain how you meet the legitimate counterarguments, you are simplistic, and your opinions are of no interest—and in a politician, especially a candidate for the presidency, potentially dangerous.

Samel continues: "Slater's perspective clearly assumes the awful premise of American exceptionalism, that the US is entitled to take actions that would be forbidden to other nations, because of our superior military capability, our superior morality, or both."

I assume no such thing. Since Samel knows and acknowledges that I opposed the Vietnam War, the Iraq War of 2003 and its continuation through the present, the Afghanistan war after al-Qaeda was defeated, and any attack on Iran, it is rather quaint of him to conclude that my view is that the US is morally entitled to do anything it wishes.

I would have thought that my actual position would have been clear by now: all wars, including those initiated by the US, must be judged by the moral principles embodied in just war moral philosophy. Some wars are justified by those criteria, most are not. This has nothing whatever to do with "American exceptionalism," unless I was arguing that the U.S, because of its superior morality and military power, should not be bound by just war principles. I'm sure Samel, when he thinks it over, will concede that I make no such argument, that in fact it is the very opposite of what I believe and have repeatedly argued.

There's yet another problem with the notion of American "exceptionalism." In several of the cases under discussion here—the US interventions in Bosnia, Kosovo, and Libya—the interventions were far from unilateral. On the contrary, they were not only supported by most western states, a number of them actively participated, and in the case of Libya, provided the main military forces.

Civilian casualties. Samel writes: "Slater acknowledges that all wars cause civilian casualties. True, but isn't that a reason to oppose almost all wars, with very very few exceptions for cases like WWII?"

I don't "acknowledge" that all wars cause civilian casualties—that's like acknowledging that the sun rises in the morning. What I argue—rather, what just war moral philosophy argues—is that the existence of civilian casualties, by itself, does not necessarily demonstrate that no wars are justified. Indeed, Samel picks the very worse case, given his position, to make his own argument: World War II. Why? Because even Samel acknowledges, though in as backhanded a way as he can, that WWII was justified. Yet, WWII without a doubt caused far more civilian casualties than any war since.

And I don't mean only German or Japanese civilian casualties. The liberation of France has been estimated to have resulted in over 60,000 deaths and 100,000 injuries, not to mention immense destruction to civilian homes and infrastructures. Did most French people think the price was too high, and would they rather have continued under indefinite Nazi occupation? Well, at least most of the French people who weren't collaborating with Hitler.

I'll repeat the point I've made a number of times: the notion that you can decide on whether a war is justified or not by asking the families of those killed takes you nowhere—unless you think, for example, that we should have asked the families of German civilians killed in WWII, including the families of the Nazis and the SS, if they thought the Allied war to liberate Europe and destroy Nazism war was justified—and then ended the war if they voted no.

Or, take the case of Libya. The western intervention undeniably caused civilian casualties. Is there any serious doubt that the Libyan people enthusiastically welcomed the overthrow of Gaddafi? Or that the price of nonintervention would have been far greater Libyan deaths and the continuation of Gaddafi's tyranny?

In short, the existence of civilian casualties, per se, tells you nothing about the justice of the war. Then, the complexities begin: In what cause? How many civilian casualties? Is there evidence that civilians were deliberately attacked, or was every effort made to minimize the casualties? How many civilians would have died, or suffered indefinitely under tyranny (or a thousand year Nazi Reich) if there had been no military intervention? Were the principles of last resort, proportionality, distinction, and the immunity of civilians from deliberate attack observed? Could diplomacy have worked? And more.

Are you simplistic if you don't understand the need to consider such issues in making moral judgments about wars? Of course.

A last point. Samel says "Slater goes so far as to say that Bush's wars were fought with bad-intentioned imperialism, while Obama has more benign motives. But he cannot support a

Democratic President's right to military action without sanctioning a Republican's right as well."

Of course I can. The issue is not which political party makes the decision, but a proper evaluation of the validity of the decision, on the merits and irrespective of partisan politics. Bush started a war with Iraq for a number of bad reasons, lied about his true reasons (none of which could pass the just cause test), and despite the fact that his administration knew that the argument that Saddam was still seeking nuclear weapons was probably false. Obama went to war in Libya for legitimate reasons. And even though I think Obama should have gotten out of Afghanistan and Iraq a lot sooner, his failure to do so does not demonstrate "imperialist" motivations.

Life is a lot more complicated than that.

A failure to recognize the many complexities and vexing issues inherent in war-and-peace issues is, indeed: "simplistic." Maybe even "simpleminded."

Attackers Argue for Use of Human Shields to Deflect Responsibility

Beth Van Schaack

In the following viewpoint, Beth Van Schaack calls attention to the use of human shields, prohibited by international humanitarian law, to gain military advantage. She argues against the manipulation of established laws by parties seeking this advantage. She acknowledges the temptation to do so, but recommends instead that proportional damage be calculated to minimize civilian deaths. Van Schaack is a former professor of human rights at the Stanford University Law School. She consults to a variety of human rights organizations, including the International Justice Resource Center.

As you read, consider the following questions:

1. Are human shields allowed according to international humanitarian law?
2. How did the human shield issue arise in Sri Lanka?
3. What is proportionality as it relates to civilian deaths?

The phenomenon of human shields challenges core tenets of international humanitarian law (IHL), including its careful dialectic between the imperatives of humanity and military

"Symposium on Critical Perspectives on Human Shields: Complementary Duties Under IHL," by Beth Van Schaack, American Society of International Law and Beth Van Schaack, 2016. https://www.cambridge.org/core/services/aop-cambridge-core/content/view/9BEEED33AE28923975BCED78F08208C3/S2398772316000052a.pdf/div-class-title-human-shields-complementary-duties-under-ihl-div.pdf. Licensed under CC by 4.0 International.

necessity. Although the principles of distinction, precaution, and proportionality are well established in the abstract, consensus remains elusive when these concepts are applied to situations involving human shields, who blur the boundary between civilians and combatants. And while the prohibition against using human shields is absolute, it is too often honored in its breach in today's asymmetrical conflicts.[1] Indeed, resort to human shields has become attractive precisely because it exploits protective legal rules to the detriment of those principled armed actors who value—and thus strive for—IHL compliance. These parties, in turn, are struggling to adapt their operations to a practice that has become "endemic" in the modern battlefield.[2]

Like other law-of-war practices, human shielding has become the subject of intense lawfare. In today's conflicts, the prohibition on the use of human shields is being cynically deployed to shield attackers from responsibility for civilian deaths. In an effort to eliminate the tactical and legal advantages that parties gain from using human shields, a range of implicated actors and norm entrepreneurs are manipulating IHL rules in ways that undermine the principle of proportionality, the presumption of civilian status, the prohibition on reprisals against protected persons, and the imperative of civilian protection. In particular, in response to the unlawful use of human shields, parties on the attack are all too liberally denying the civilian character of any of the shields in order to avoid having to consider their presence in prestrike determinations of proportionality. These schemes, however, have no basis in treaty law or in authoritative articulations of customary international law (CIL) and will do little to deter unscrupulous parties willing to use human shields in the first place. As such, efforts to "relax" or alter the principle of proportionality and the presumption of civilian status, even in the face of blatant violations of the human shields prohibition by a ruthless adversary, should be rejected. The right approach is to hold all sides to their IHL obligations, which in the case of human shields, are complementary and mutually reinforcing.

Human Shields in Sri Lanka

This instrumentalization of the prohibition on human shields is exemplified in the competing narratives around civilian casualties stemming from the civil war in Sri Lanka, where the Liberation Tigers of Tamil Eelam's (LTTE) strategic, and despicable, manipulation of the Tamil civilian population has been trotted out in defense of the government's deliberate, indiscriminate, and disproportionate attacks on civilians. By all accounts, the ending of the civil war in Sri Lanka was brutal and there were no angels in that fight. In the final weeks of the twenty-five year conflict, upwards of forty thousand civilians may have been killed in the Vanni war zone during the fateful last stand of the LTTE.[3] Not surprisingly, the parties differ on where to place the blame for the carnage.

To hear the triumphant government tell it, the LTTE took thousands of civilians hostage, deployed the civilian population as human shields around LTTE cadre and assets, attacked anyone trying to flee towards government created "No Fire Zones" (NFZ); and embedded themselves in civilian areas, including NFZs, in order either to shield themselves or to draw government fire. By contrast, Tamil survivors tell a story of the government promising civilians immunity from attack and herding them toward the NFZs, but then bombarding these putative safe zones with heavy artillery notwithstanding its claimed "zero civilian casualty" policy. In defense of its own actions, the government has claimed that Tamil civilians were being "held hostage"—potentially to inspire international intervention on their behalf—and that the security forces were engaged in humanitarian operations with the goal of "liberating them."[4] To the extent that they acknowledge civilian deaths, government sources shift all responsibility to the LTTE, arguing that any harm to civilians was the result of the LTTE's "cynical choice of tactics."[5]

Independent inquiries by UN investigators, journalists, independent nongovernmental organizations, and human rights groups have criticized both sides for their conduct during the war. The UN Secretary-General's Panel of Experts condemned the government for deliberately shelling NFZs, food distribution lines, and hospitals.[6] It also extensively documented the LTTE's violations of the principle of distinction (including the creation of "human buffers"), and their forced recruitment of civilians and child soldiers. The UN High Commissioner of Human Right's Independent Investigation on Sri Lanka documented a range of IHL abuses on the part of the government, including the use of direct and indirect fire against its NFZs.[7] Even the government's own Lessons Learnt and Reconciliation Commission (LLRC) took the bold and welcome step of acknowledging that government fire into civilian areas harmed civilians[8] (a departure from the standard government line).

In response to international efforts to document IHL violations during the war, the prior government of Sri Lanka convened a number of its own competing commissions of inquiry. Leaked copies of what purport to be the work product of American and European international law consultants to these bodies later appeared on various Sri Lankan websites. Neither the provenance nor authenticity of these analyses have been verified, and they are stripped of their footnotes, so it is impossible to verify the sources of authority cited. Regardless of whether these documents are what they purport to be, they exhibit a range of arguments using the presence of even involuntary human shields to justify reducing the legal obligations of the attacking party. Collectively, these analyses assert that breaches of the principle of distinction by the LTTE fully absolve the government of Sri Lanka of any responsibility for harm to civilians such that the LTTE should "bear the principle liability for civilian casualties" during the final stages of the war.[9] These conclusions are reached by manipulating the IHL principle of proportionality and the rule on precautions, ignoring the presumption of civilian status, and misusing the concepts of reciprocity and reprisals. The remainder of this piece will outline the specifics of each analytical flaw.

Proportionality & the Civilian Presumption under Attack

According to the proportionality principle, whenever civilians or civilian objects are in the vicinity of a military objective, attacks are prohibited if they "may be expected to cause incidental loss of civilian life, injury to civilians, damage to civilian objects, or a combination thereof, which would be excessive in relation to the concrete and direct military advantage anticipated." As an independent duty, parties must take "all feasible precautions" to spare civilian lives, including by issuing effective advance warnings if practicable. In cases of doubt, CIL (mirroring Additional Protocol I to the Geneva Conventions) establishes a presumption of civilian status in all conflicts.

Black letter IHL would dictate that human shields enjoy these protections so long as they are not deemed to be directly participating in hostilities (DPH). Although the law is inconclusive as to when voluntary human shields are deemed to be DPH, the relevant rules are highly settled as regards involuntary shields, who are entitled to immunity from direct attack and protection from incidental harm afforded by the principle of proportionality.[10] In other words, involuntary human shields must be treated like all other civilians. As such, individuals who are inadvertent or coerced shields continue to enjoy immunity from direct, indiscriminate, and disproportionate attacks—i.e., from intentional and incidental harm.

By contrast, the leaked texts overstate the degree of legal indeterminacy in this area and advance a range of alternative theories that manipulate the relative significance of the two elements of proportionality. When it comes to the weight accorded to human shields on the civilian side of the calculus, the opinions posit that the principle of proportionality either does not apply at all[11] or should be adjusted to account for the fact that the LTTE used human shields—whether voluntary or involuntary—to its advantage.[12] Accordingly, it is argued that the government should be given a "margin of latitude commensurate with the military exigencies that they encountered and taking into account the widespread unlawful use of civilians by the LTTE."[13] Indeed, it is claimed that the government could undertake "a marked adjustment in the 'proportionality' calculation" given the LTTE's widespread policy of using civilian shields and the rebels' "past conduct" in exposing innocent civilians to the dangers of armed conflict.[14]

These statements completely elide the important legal distinction between voluntary and involuntary shields[15] by treating those willing confederates who choose to participate in the conflict the same as those civilians who have been "deprived of their physical freedom of action [and] physically coerced into providing cover in close combat."[16] Because voluntariness is deemed impossible to verify, the analyses conclude that the risk of civilian casualties is essentially unknowable and thus need not be taken into account at all.[17] By contrast, IHL demands that parties must suspend or cancel an attack that cannot adhere to the proportionality test. As such, any lack of certainty cannot eliminate or diminish the protections that are afforded. Furthermore, none of these analyses acknowledges the presumption of civilian status, which would require an attacking party to treat all human shields as civilians in the absence of adequate proof to the contrary. The leaked texts effectively invert this presumption, arguing that because it is difficult to determine whether the shields are operating voluntarily or are coerced, the government was entitled to ignore or discount their presence.

On the other side of the proportionality ledger is the military advantage to be gained by the attacker. The reports cite the overarching goal of defeating the LTTE in order to end the conflict as a factor to be weighed against the risk of harm to civilians. Thus, it is argued, "the termination of such insidious and wholesale threats to civilian life represents a compelling military objective which already sets the bar fairly high relative to the acceptable level of civilian casualties in achieving that objective."[18] Accordingly, one report argues that even assuming forty thousand civilians (12 percent) were killed in the final offensive, over 295,000 civilians were "saved" by the governmental operations in question, rendering it a "successful operation."[19] The inflated military advantage of "winning" could justify even excessive collateral damage, overwhelm any IHL analysis, and render proportionality little more than an exercise in the end justifying the means.[20] The law actually requires that the military advantage be assessed with respect to a particular engagement or attack at the tactical or operational level and not to the goals of the entire campaign or conflict, writ large. Nor can the advantage be speculative or too remote.

To be sure, the drafters of the Statute of the International Criminal Court added the word "overall" before "military advantage" and "clearly" before "excessive," when it comes to assigning criminal liability before that institution; and, some states have entered treaty reservations to the effect that "the military advantage anticipated from an attack is intended to refer to the advantage anticipated from the attack considered as a whole and not only from isolated or particular parts of the attack."[21] Nonetheless, the ultimate strategic goal of prevailing in the conflict or the generalized objective of halting all IHL breaches by an adversary are too amorphous and remote to serve as weighable factors in a rigorous proportionality analysis, which requires a consideration of the "concrete and direct military advantage anticipated."

The Ban on Reprisals Against Civilians & the Irrelevance of Reciprocity

The goals of ending violations of IHL by the LTTE—including but not limited to the use of human shields— and of "rescuing" civilians trapped behind the front lines[22] are also cited as "military advantages" to be considered in calculating whether a planned attack will be proportionate.[23] The objective of ending the LTTE's IHL breaches as relevant to measuring proportionality sounds of collective punishments[24] and reprisals. As one leaked analysis argues:

> In psychological terms, the Sri Lanka strikes directed at military objectives, despite the presence of human shields should be categorized as a form of positive punishment designed to end the unwanted behavior.[25]

Reprisals—otherwise unlawful acts that are allowed as a last resort if committed in response to a breach by an adversary with the goal of bringing that party back into compliance—are prohibited against protected persons under IHL, including civilians.[26] To be sure, the ICRC considers this CIL rule to be applicable only in international armed conflicts,[27] but there is little justification for not applying this rule across the conflict spectrum.[28] An even broader ban on reprisals against civilians finds support from the Vienna Convention on the Law of Treaties, which states that a material breach of humanitarian treaty provisions dedicated to "the protection of the human person" does not entitle the other party to suspend its own obligations, particularly when it comes to any form of reprisals against persons protected by such treaties.[29]

Even when the defending party is in breach of these rules, the attacking party remains subject to its own IHL obligations vis-à-vis the shields.[30] It is axiomatic that reciprocity plays no role in determining whether a party must obey IHL, and tu quoque is no longer a viable defense.[31] As such, the attacker's obligations are owed erga omnes and remain intact even in the face of breaches by the adversary and even though the defender violates IHL.[32] The law would be perverse indeed if it were to allow the attacker to "punish" the party using human shields by attacking those very shields.

There is an obvious appeal to assigning the responsibility of any civilian deaths to the party originally placing those civilians at risk. The defender's IHL duty to protect civilians under its control is a pressing one that deserves robust enforcement. There is no question that the international community should endeavor to develop and strengthen the norm against using, or benefiting from, the conduct of human shields, whether voluntary or involuntary. This norm should be enforced through the apportionment of both state responsibility and individual criminal responsibility as well as through diplomatic action in nonjudicial fora. In the event that civilians are harmed in an armed conflict, it is not a binary question of allocating all responsibility to one party or another. Rather, liability can be shared by, and apportioned across, multiple actors through principles of comparative fault familiar from domestic tort law. Accordingly, the LTTE's rampant violations of the principle of distinction did not suspend or alter the Sri Lankan government's obligations, which remained intact and fully enforceable against it. The duties of the attacking and the defending parties are complementary and both should be scrupulously enforced in this deadly dyad, even if we may agree that the ultimate responsibility from a moral sense resides with the party willing to use civilians to shield otherwise lawful military objectives.

Conclusion

The reports ostensibly produced for the Government of Sri Lanka reveal the way in which the prohibition on the use of human shields can be manipulated to the detriment of those civilians it is designed to protect. To be sure, one must acknowledge the profound difficulties faced by field commanders confronting an adversary actively breaching the principle of distinction by using civilians as human shields, or otherwise taking advantage of the civilian presence in order to screen its activities. In light of the many ways that coercion can operate in situations of armed conflict, it is virtually impossible to verify agency, particularly from the perspective of a targeteer or military lawyer committed to conducting a genuine collateral damage estimate. However, this is precisely where the presumption of civilian status—as a binding rule and prudential practice—provides clarity and a legitimate course of action.

Moreover, it is tempting to insist that the law should deprive a party benefiting from the presence of human shields, and the immunity they rightfully enjoy, of its unjust advantage. Otherwise, it is argued, IHL will punish a party in compliance for the adversary's criminality. Legal rules don't work this way, however. There are many real-world factors that intervene to stymie otherwise lawful attacks—bad weather, poor infrastructure, imperfect equipment, etc. The architects of IHL had to choose: either hamstring an attacker in the presence of human shields or sacrifice civilians to enable an attack against a proper military objective to go forward. They chose to do the former. Parties confronting human shields must thus treat this inhumane tactic as another obstacle to be lawfully surmounted on the modern battlefield.

Given the difficulty of ensuring voluntariness, the safest course for parties truly committed to the values underlying IHL and for lawyers advising embattled clients is to treat all human shields as civilians when it comes to calculating acceptable (i.e., proportional) collateral damage, unless there is irrefutable proof of willing participation in hostilities. This close-to-categorical approach finds support in the presumption of civilian status under IHL and the duties of warring parties to take "all feasible precautions" to protect the civilian population. To the extent that there are ambiguities in the law, resort to a teleological interpretive approach, as dictated by the Martens Clause, yields the same result. This is also the most prudent course in light of the risk that harm to individuals acting as human shields—even if technically sanctioned by the law as acceptable collateral damage—will exert a high political cost and offer a propaganda windfall to the adversary. Furthermore, respecting these constraints will not only ensure compliance with the law of armed conflict, it will also protect our war fighters' "morality [and] their ability to live with the emotional consequences of " their conduct in war.[33]

Endnotes

1. ICRC, Customary International Law Database, Rule 97.
2. Michael N. Schmitt, Human Shields in International Humanitarian Law, 38 ISR. Y.B. HUM. RTS. 17, 18 (2008).
3. Colum Lynch, U.N.: Sri Lanka's Crushing of Tamil Tigers may have killed 40,000 Civilians, WASH. POST (Apr. 21, 2011).
4. See SRI LANKA, MIN. OF DEFENSE, HUMANITARIAN OPERATION FACTUAL ANALYSIS (July 2006–May 2009).
5. FULL REPORT OF THE ARMY BOARD ON LLRC OBSERVATIONS RELEASED 4.
6. REPORT OF THE SECRETARY-GENERAL'S PANEL OF EXPERTS ON

ACCOUNTABILITY IN SRI LANKA (Mar. 31, 2011).

7. Comprehensive Report of the Office of the United Nations High Commissioner for Human Rights on Sri Lanka, UN Doc. A/HRC/ 30/61 (Sept. 28, 2015) [hereinafter "OISL Report"].

8. REPORT OF THE COMMISSION OF INQUIRY ON LESSONS LEARNT AND RECONCILIATION (Nov. 2011).

9. Leaked Memorandum dated March 18, 2016, para. 21, THE ISLAND.

10. Nils Melzer, Interpretive Guidance on the Notion of Direct Participation in Hostilities in International Humanitarian Law 56 (2009).

11. Leaked Memorandum dated March 18, 2016, supra note 9, at para. 22.

12. Leaked Memorandum dated September 28, 2014, para. 21, THE ISLAND; Leaked Memorandum dated March 10, 2015, para. 37 THE ISLAND.

13. Leaked Memorandum dated March 10, 2015, supra note 12, at para. 10.

14. Id. at para. 44 (emphasis added).

15. Public Committee Against Torture in Israel v. Israel, HCJ 769/02, para. 36 (Isr. 2005).

16. Melzer, supra note 10, at 60.

17. Leaked Memorandum dated September 28, 2014, supra note 11, at paras. 21, 43.

18. Leaked Memorandum dated March 18, 2016, supra note 9, at para. 39.

19. Id.

20. Leaked Memorandum dated March 10, 2015, supra note 12, at para. 43.

21. Declaration of the United Kingdom of Great Britain and Northern Island (July 2, 2002).

22. Leaked Memorandum dated March 18, 2016, supra note 9, at para. 43.

23. Leaked Memorandum dated March 10, 2015, supra note 12, at para. 44.

24. ICRC, supra note 1, Rule 103.

25. Leaked Memorandum dated September 28, 2014, supra note 12, at para. 21(a).

26. Protocol Additional to the Geneva Conventions of 12 August 1949, and relating to the Protection of Victims of International Armed Conflicts art. 51, June 8, 1977, 1125 UNTS 3 [hereinafter Protocol I].

27. ICRC, supra note 1, Rule 146. See Article 3(2) Protocol (II) on Prohibitions or Restrictions on the Use of Mines, Booby-Traps and Other Devices art. 3(2), May 3, 1996, 1342 UNTS 168 (1983) (prohibiting reprisals against civilians).

28. Prosecutor v. Kupreškić, Case No. IT-95-16-T, Judgement, paras. 513, 527–36 (Jan. 14, 2000).

29. Vienna Convention on the Law of Treaties art. 5, May 23, 1969, 1155 UNTS 331.

30. OISL Report, supra note 7, at para. 764.

31. ICRC, supra note 1, Rule 140.

32. Protocol I, supra note 26, art. 51; ICRC, supra note 1, Rule 22.

33. Chris Jenks, Moral Touchstone, not General Deterrence: The Role of International Criminal Justice in Fostering Compliance with International Humanitarian Law, 96 ICRC REV. 776, 782 (2014).

President Trump Speaks Out Against Death of Innocent Civilians in the Middle East

Russia Matters

In the following viewpoint, President Trump's statements about NATO-Russia relations, the conflict in Syria, counterterrorism, Ukraine, and relations with Russia articulate a desire to save both military and civilian lives. He specifically cites the high civilian death toll among Arabs and Muslims in Middle Eastern countries. He refers to words and actions the United States must take to enact a cease-fire in Syria and fight against terrorism. These statements are presented as media snippets published by the press. Russia Matters is a project by Harvard Kennedy School's Belfer Center for Science and International Affairs whose aim is to improve the understanding of the US-Russian relationship among America's policymakers.

As you read, consider the following questions:

1. In which statements does President Trump contradict himself?
2. What does President Trump want Russia to stop doing?
3. What did President Trump call the shooting of Russia's ambassador in Ankara?

"Trump on Russia: Insights and Recommendations," Russia Matters, July 20, 2017. Reprinted by permission.

Military Issues, including NATO-Russia Relations

September 2016: During the presidential debates, Trump said the US need to upgrade its nuclear arsenal as part of having a strong military. "Russia has been expanding their—they have a much newer capability than we do. We have not been updating from the new standpoint," Trump said. (*New York Times*, 09.26.16)

Later, Trump was asked to comment on reports that then-President Obama was considering changing longstanding US nuclear policy by declaring a "No First Use" policy. "I would like everybody to end it, just get rid of it. But I would certainly not do first strike. I think that once the nuclear alternative happens, it's over," he said. "At the same time, we have to be prepared. I can't take anything off the table." (*The Washington Post*, 09.28.16)

October 2016: At the second presidential debate on Oct. 9, Trump said, "Russia is new in terms of nuclear. We are old. We're tired. We're exhausted in terms of nuclear. A very bad thing." (*New York Times*, 10.10.16)

"We're in very serious trouble, because we have a country with tremendous numbers of nuclear warheads—1,800, by the way—where they [Russians] expanded and we didn't, 1,800 nuclear warheads," Trump said at the final presidential debate on Oct. 19. (Real Clear Politics, 10.19.16)

[…]

January 2017: Trump called NATO "obsolete because it wasn't taking care of terror" and said member organizations aren't paying their "fair share." Trump also said that the "U.K. was so smart in getting out" of the EU, which he described as "a vehicle for Germany." Germany's Foreign Minister Frank-Walter Steinmeier said Trump's comments had aroused concern across the 28-member alliance. NATO reacted on Jan. 16 to Trump's statement by saying it has full confidence in the US security commitment to Europe. In contrast, Moscow has welcomed Trump calling NATO "obsolete." Russian President Vladimir Putin's spokesman, Dmitry Peskov, said on Jan. 16 that "NATO is indeed a vestige [of the past] and we agree with that." (AP, 01.15.17, *Reuters*, 01.17.17, RFE/RL, 01.16.17, *Slate*, 01.16.17)

February 2017: "We've fallen behind on nuclear weapon capacity. … It would be wonderful, a dream would be that no country would have nukes, but if countries are going to have nukes, we're going to be at the top of the pack," Trump told Reuters on Feb. 23. (*Reuters*, 02.23.17)

April 2017: Trump backtracked on his NATO comment. "I said it was obsolete. It's no longer obsolete," he said at a news conference with NATO Secretary-General Jens Stoltenberg after they met in the Oval Office. "If other countries pay their fair share instead of relying on the United States to make up the difference, we will all be much more secure and our partnership will be made that much stronger," he said. (AP, 04.13.17, *Bloomberg*, 04.12.17)

[…]

July 2017: In a speech in Warsaw, Trump vowed to confront "new forms of aggression" targeting the West and called for Moscow to stop fomenting unrest around the world. He warned that Western interests were being tested by "propaganda, financial crimes and cyber warfare," forcing NATO to adapt. "We urge Russia to cease its destabilizing activities in Ukraine and elsewhere, and its support for hostile regimes including Syria and Iran, and to join the community of responsible nations in our fight against common enemies and in defense of civilization itself," he said. His speech, which came ahead of the G20 summit meeting in Hamburg, included an explicit commitment to Article 5: "The United States has demonstrated not merely with words, but with its actions, that we stand firmly behind Article 5, the mutual defense commitment," he said. In the speech, Trump also described Poland as an exemplary ally in building defenses to counter Russian "destabilizing behavior." (*Bloomberg*, 07.06.17, AP, 06.07.17, *Reuters*, 07.06.15)

[…]

Conflict in Syria

April 2017: Following his decision to launch of barrage of missiles at a Syrian airfield over Assad's suspected use of chemical weapons, Trump said in an interview with the Fox Business Network: "I see them using gas ... we have to do something." Trump called Assad "an animal" and "truly an evil person," and he said that it is now up to Putin to withdraw his support for the Syrian regime. Trump also provided additional insight into his reasoning: "What I did should have been done by the Obama Administration a long time before I did it, and you would have had a much better—I think Syria would be a lot better off right now than it has been." At the same time, Trump said he wouldn't intervene militarily against Assad unless the Syrian leader resorts to using weapons of mass destruction again. "Are we going to get involved with Syria? No," Trump said. (*The Washington Post*, 04.12.17, *The Washington Post*, 04.12.17, AP, 04.13.17)

May 2017: The White House issued a statement on May 2, after Trump and Putin had their first phone call since the US strike in Syria: "President Trump and President Putin agreed that the suffering in Syria has gone on for far too long and that all parties must do all they can to end the violence." (*The Washington Post*, 05.02.17)

July 2017: Trump touted a Syria ceasefire deal that came out of his first face-to-face meeting with Putin at the G20 summit in Hamburg. "We negotiated a ceasefire in parts of Syria which will save lives. Now it is time to move forward in working constructively with Russia!" Trump tweeted. (CNN, 07.08.17, Twitter, 07.09.17)

Trump said that he was in talks with Russia to extend the ceasefire across more territory in Syria. "By having some commutations and dialogue, we are able to have a ceasefire and it is going to go on for a while and frankly, we are working on a second ceasefire in a very rough part of Syria," he said at a news conference in Paris. (CNN, 07.13.17)

Donald Trump Uses the Final Presidential Debate to Talk about ISIS

When Donald Trump finds himself with a debate question he doesn't like, he deploys a simple strategy: Talk about ISIS.

Like a labyrinth with many entrances but only one exit, Trump managed to steer his answers back to a dubious theme he's seized on, that ISIS is a creation of the Obama administration, when Hillary Clinton served as US secretary of state. The claim has been debunked—in part because the terrorist group's roots date to 2004, before Obama's election—but it hasn't stopped Trump from returning to it again and again.

On the topic of economic plans, Trump responded to a jab from Clinton about taking money from his father by abruptly changing the subject: "I started with a $1 million dollar loan. I agree with that—$1 million dollar loan. But I built a phenomenal company. And if we could run our country the way I've run my company, we would have a country that you will be so proud of. You would even be proud of it. And frankly, when you look at her real record, take a look at Syria. Take a look at the migration. Take a look at Libya. Take a look at Iraq. She gave us ISIS because her and Obama created this huge vacuum."

After an attack by Clinton for his admiration of Russian president Vladimir Putin, Trump steered his answer to ISIS. (Cooperating with Russia on attacks on ISIS "would be good," he said.)

And when the subject was his record of groping women, Trump expressed his wish to return to his preferred subject: "The other things are false but honestly I'd love to talk about getting rid of ISIS and I'd love to talk about other things."

Trump's ISIS tactic isn't new— he tried the same thing at the second debate, when he was asked about his comments on assaulting women— but it probably wasn't any more effective tonight.

"At the final presidential debate, Donald Trump steered every question he could back to ISIS," by Oliver Staley, Quartz Media LLC, October 19, 2016.

Counterterrorism

December 2016: Following the assassination of Russia's ambassador in Ankara, Putin vowed to step up the fight against terrorism.

Trump called the shooting "a violation of all rules of civilized order." (*Bloomberg*, 12.20.16)

[…]

May 2017: In a speech on global terrorism he gave while visiting Saudi Arabia, Trump said: "Few nations have been spared the violent reach of terrorism. America has suffered repeated barbaric attacks… The nations of Europe have also endured unspeakable horror. So too have the nations of Africa and South America. India, Russia, China and Australia have all been victims. But in sheer numbers, the deadliest toll has been exacted on the innocent people of Arab, Muslim and Middle Eastern nations." (*The Washington Post*, 05.21.17)

[…]

Ukraine

March 2016: As a presidential candidate, Trump expressed wariness about US involvement in the Ukraine conflict. "I look at the Ukraine situation and I say, so Ukraine is a country that affects us far less than it affects other countries in NATO, and yet we are doing all of the lifting, they're not doing anything. And I say, why is it that Germany is not dealing with NATO on Ukraine? Why is it that other countries that are in the vicinity of the Ukraine not dealing with—why are we always the one that's leading, potentially the third world war, okay, with Russia?" (*The Washington Post*, 03.22.16).

During a Republican debate, Trump said: "You have countries that surround Ukraine. They don't talk. They don't seem to have a problem. I'm not saying go in. I'd say be very strong, you can be strong without necessarily even being (inaudible) or the money we spend," he said. (CNN, 03.29.16)

[…]

August 2016: At a campaign stop, Trump said the US would trigger a third world war if they were to retake Crimea for Ukraine. "I know it [the annexation] exactly. That was two years ago. I mean, do you want to go back, do you want to have World War III to get it back?" he said. (*Newsweek*, 08.02.16)

February 2017: President Trump said he did not take offense at the outbreak of a lethal bout of fighting in Ukraine that began within a day of his phone conversation with Putin, saying of the recent clashes, "We don't really know exactly what that is." In a Fox News interview, Trump said of the Ukrainian separatists, "They're pro forces... We don't know, are they uncontrollable? Are they uncontrolled? That happens also. We're going to find out; I would be surprised, but we'll see." (*New York Times*, 02.06.17).

[...]

June 2017: Following a White House meeting with Ukrainian President Petro Poroshenko, Trump said Ukraine is a "place that we've all been very much involved in." He added, "We've had some very, very good discussions. It's going to continue throughout the day and I think a lot of progress has been made." The meeting coincided with the decision of the US Treasury Department to expand existing sanctions on Russia over its military involvement in Ukraine, which, the department said, "will remain in place until Russia fully honors its obligations under the Minsk Agreements," while measures "related to Crimea will not be lifted until Russia ends its occupation of the peninsula." (*Bloomberg*, 06.20.17)

July 2017: In a speech in Warsaw, Trump urged Russia to "cease its destabilizing activities in Ukraine." (White House, 07.06.17)

In an interview with the New York Times he said: "Don't forget, Crimea was given away during Obama. Not during Trump. ... Crimea was gone during the Obama administration, and he gave, he allowed it to get away." (*New York Times*, 07.19.17)

[...]

Bilateral Relations and Russia in General

March 2014: In a series of interviews, Donald Trump singled out Russia as the United States' "biggest problem" and greatest geopolitical foe. In the interviews reviewed by CNN from March 2014, which aired on NBC News and Fox News, Trump goes as far as to suggest imposing sanctions to hurt Russia economically and then later says he supports such sanctions. Trump also expressed his agreement with Mitt Romney's 2012 assessment that Russia is the United States' number one "geopolitical foe." (CNN, 01.17.17)

April 2016: In a much-anticipated foreign policy speech, Trump expressed hope about the potential for improvement in American-Russian relations: "We desire to live peacefully and in friendship with Russia and China. We have serious differences with these two nations, and must regard them with open eyes. But we are not bound to be adversaries. We should seek common ground based on shared interests. Russia, for instance, has also seen the horror of Islamic terrorism. I believe an easing of tensions and improved relations with Russia—from a position of strength—is possible. Common sense says this cycle of hostility must end. Some say the Russians won't be reasonable. I intend to find out. If we can't make a good deal for America, then we will quickly walk from the table." (*Washington Examiner*, 04.27.17)

July 2016: "I would love to have a good relationship where Russia and I, instead of, and us, and the US, instead of fighting each other we got along. It would be wonderful if we had good relationships with Russia so that we don't have to go through all of the drama," Trump said. (*New York Times*, 07.21.16)

September 2016: "Only the out-of-touch media elites think the biggest problems facing America—you know this, this is what they talk about, facing American society today is that there are 11 million illegal immigrants who don't have legal status. And, they also think the biggest thing, and you know this, it's not nuclear, and it's not ISIS, it's not Russia, it's not China, it's global warming," Trump said in a speech on immigration. (Cox Media, 09.01.16)

[...]

November 2016: In their first direct phone call, lasting 30 minutes, Trump and Putin reportedly discussed the "highly dissatisfactory" state of US-Russian relations, as well as the need to take steps to "normalize" ties and undertake "constructive cooperation on a wide range of issues," including the fight against international terrorism and extremism, according to an official statement released by the Kremlin. The two men also reportedly discussed the armed crisis in Syria. Trump's office later said that Putin had called to "offer his congratulations" and that they had discussed shared threats and challenges, "strategic economic issues" and the long-term relationship between the two nations. Trump told Putin "that he is very much looking forward to having a strong and enduring relationship with Russia and the People of Russia." The Kremlin said Trump and Putin both agreed to remain in regular telephone contact, and begin planning for a future meeting in person. (*The Moscow Times*, 11.15.16, *Reuters*, 11.15.16, *Wall Street Journal*, 11.11.16, *The Moscow Times*, 11.14.16, *The Washington Post*, 11.14.16, *Wall Street Journal*, 11.17.16, *Bloomberg*, 11.17.16)

[…]

March 2017: Trump again accused former President Obama of being too weak on Russia, saying Moscow "got stronger and stronger" during his tenure. "For eight years Russia 'ran over' President Obama, got stronger and stronger, picked-off Crimea and added missiles. Weak!" Trump tweeted. (*The Hill*, 03.07.17)

April 2017: At a news conference at the White House, Trump acknowledged that relations between the US and Russia "may be at an all-time low," but said he remained optimistic that the US and its allies "could get along with Russia." "Based on everything I'm hearing, things went pretty well, maybe better than anticipated," he said of Rex Tillerson's Moscow visit, in which the secretary of state and his Russian counterpart vented deep disagreements during hours of talks. "Things will work out fine between the U.S.A. and Russia," Trump tweeted. "At the right time everyone will come to their senses & there will be lasting peace!" (*Bloomberg*, 04.12.17)

July 2017: In a far-reaching interview with the *New York Times*, Trump also mentioned: Allegations of the Clintons' relationship with Russia: "Hillary did the reset. Somebody was saying today, and then I read, where Hillary Clinton was dying to get back with Russia. Her husband made a speech, got half a million bucks [from Russia] while she was secretary of state. She did the uranium deal, which is a horrible thing, while she was secretary of state, and got a lot of money." (*New York Times*, 07.19.17)

Russia's history of war: Napoleon's "one problem is he didn't go to Russia that night because he had extracurricular activities, and they [the French] froze to death. How many times has Russia been saved by the weather? ... Same thing happened to Hitler. Not for that reason, though. Hitler wanted to consolidate. He was all set to walk in. But he wanted to consolidate, and it went and dropped to 35 degrees below zero, and that was the end of that army. ... But the Russians have great fighters in the cold. They use the cold to their advantage. I mean, they've won five wars where the armies that went against them froze to death. ... It's pretty amazing." (*New York Times*, 07.19.17)

In Egypt, a Rise in Civilian Casualties Fuels Anti-Government Sentiment

Maged Mandour

In the following viewpoint, Maged Mandour argues that Egyptian state-sanctioned heavy weaponry and airstrikes giving rise to civilian casualties are ineffective and are angering the population against the military. He cites a number of instances where village civilians were killed. He recommends that the central government collaborate with local tribes in its counterterrorism campaigns. Mandour is a political analyst specializing in Egyptian affairs. He writes for the Carnegie Endowment for International Peace's online Sada Journal.

As you read, consider the following questions:

1. What is the goal of the Egyptian military in Sinai?
2. What military strategies are contributing to the increase in civilian deaths?
3. What kind of strike killed ten people during Friday prayer in the city of Rafah?

As the Egyptian military struggles to contain the Islamic State (IS) affiliate in Sinai, Wilayat Sinai, its already forceful response is becoming more heavy-handed. Increased reliance on

"The Heavy Civilian Toll in Sinai," by Maged Mandour, Sada Journal, Carnegie Endowment for International Peace, March 16, 2017. Reprinted by permission.

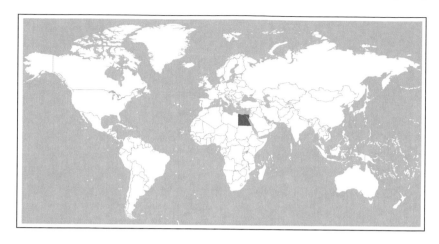

heavy weaponry and air power is contributing to a rise in civilian causalities and inflaming anti-government sentiment.

Extrajudicial killings in Sinai increased in 2016, according to the Nadeem Center for Rehabilitation of Victims of Violence, reaching 1,234 out of 1,384 extrajudicial killings across the country, constituting 89.2 percent of all cases documented. Within that, the vast majority of cases (1,177) occurred in the North Sinai province, which includes the towns of al-Arish and Shiekh Zuweid, as well as Halal Mountain, the epicenter of the insurgency. Across Egypt, air raids were responsible for 451 of the cases reported, assassinations for 443 cases, deaths during sustained state operations for 368 cases, and artillery for 56 cases. The use of artillery and the air force therefore constitute 36.6 percent of all extrajudicial killing in Egypt. By comparison, in 2015, the total number of extrajudicial killings reached 328 nationwide, with air power and artillery claiming the lives of 43 individuals combined, or 13.1 percent of the total death toll.

Reflecting the heavier crackdown is a rise in the number of attacks claimed by Wilayat Sinai, the local IS affiliate and the main insurgent group, reaching 48 attacks per month for the first six months of 2016, compared to 28 per month for the six months prior. Still, the rise in terrorist attacks does not entirely explain the increase in state-sanctioned civilian deaths to the extent the

Egypt President Stresses No Civilian Casualties

Egyptian President Abdel-Fattah El-Sisi said in a TV phone interview on Monday that Egypt's ongoing fight against terrorism in Sinai is taking a heavy toll on the state's resources.

In a phone interview with TV host Amr Adib on his late night show Kol Youm on ONTV channel, El-Sisi said that the cost of fighting terrorism has been "huge" over the last three-and-a-half years, not only in "sacrifices made through the blood of our children, but also in the monetary cost."

The president's phone interview came hours after two terrorist attacks in North Sinai's El-Arish killed eight security personnel and one civilian and injured dozens more.

El-Sisi said there are currently 41 army battalions of up to 25,000 personnel fighting in North Sinai alongside the police, which he says takes heavy resources to maintain.

"The fight against terrorism does not end in one or two days, and [we] are committing a lot of [our] resources to just being ready [for a possible terrorist attack]," he said.

The president also stressed that that the army is careful to ensure there are no civilian casualties in its anti-terror operations in Sinai.

"The people living in Sheikh Zuweid, Rafah and El-Arish should not pay the price [for what is happening in Sinai]," El-Sisi said.

The president also said that Egypt is facing terrorism alone on behalf of the entire world, and that when "the entire region has been moving in a direction in accordance with a plot being executed, only Egyptians decided to move in a different direction."

"In Sinai, you are talking about a plot and resources being [provided to militants by] certain countries and apparatuses. These are whom I refer to as the people of evil," El-Sisi said, adding that over the last three months, millions of dollars and Egyptian pounds, as well as 1,000 tonnes of explosives, were confiscated from hideouts in North Sinai.

However, the president declined to name any specific countries that might be behind this "plot."

He also said that "the new US administration has said that Egypt is the only state fighting terrorism with courage, strength and honesty," adding that the region would not have been able to withstand the threat of terrorism if Egypt were not in this fight.

"Egypt's counterterrorism efforts taking toll on state resources: Sisi," Ahram Online,
January 10, 2017.

scorched-earth tactics of the Egyptian military do. For example, based on local reports from September 2015, entire villages associated with the militants were wiped out by heavy shelling, including the villages of al-Touma, al-Mahdiya, al-Moqataa, and al-Goura, among others. There are also local reports of direct shooting at civilian homes; when residents complain to authorities, the military accuses them of having ties with the militants. Moreover, there are local reports of attacks by the Egyptian air force on villages in Sinai, leading to the destruction of a number of homes and civilian deaths.

In addition, the number of casualties during counterterrorism operations far exceeds the estimated number of Wilayat Sinai fighters. Since the start of the large counterterrorism "Operation Martyr's Right" in September 2015, the Egyptian military has reported that 2,529 militants were killed and 2,481 others arrested as of December 2016. However, foreign intelligence agencies, including the Central Intelligence Agency (CIA) and the Israel Defense Forces, estimated in mid-2016 that the size of Wilayat Sinai ranges from several hundred to a thousand militants, far below the numbers of reported killings. This disconnect can be explained by faulty intelligence or by inflating of the number of militants killed to include civilian deaths among militant deaths. The Egyptian government has a history of attacking civilians mistaken for militants. Local sources in Sinai back up the existence of such incidents, including an invented attack on a police station in Sheikh Zuweid that was used to justify the deaths of civilians in September 2013.

The counterinsurgency operation has increasingly been undifferentiated in its targeting of the local population. On January 13, five local youth were assassinated who were accused of being part of an attack on a police checkpoint that claimed the lives of eight policemen. In response, the local Bedouin tribes around the city of al-Arish launched a limited civil disobedience campaign to placate the public, refusing to pay water and electricity bills on February 11. The families claimed that at the time of the attack on the checkpoint, the five youth were already being held by state security forces, specifically the national security agency. This is not the first time that Egyptian security forces have been accused of executing defendants already in custody at the time of their alleged crimes, the most notable example of which is the case of Arab Sharkas. Six men were executed after being accused of killing soldiers during a Wilayat Sinai raid on the village of Arab Sharkas in March 2014, even though there was strong evidence that they were under arrest at the time the raid was committed.

Other cases, documented by a local NGO called Sinai for Human Rights, indicate more deliberate extrajudicial killings of civilians in recent months. Four civilians were publicly assassinated following their arrest on January 27, 2017, the motivation for which remains unclear. There are also a number of documented cases of civilian deaths at security checkpoints and more frequent cases where air strikes and heavy weaponry killed civilians. For example, on January 20, a drone strike killed ten civilians attending Friday prayers in the south of the city of Rafah. The same month, an artillery shell fell on residential area in the south of al-Arish, killing three civilians, including two children.

State-sanctioned violence against civilians has only increased local anger against the military, whose actions have also led to the deterioration of the local living conditions by imposing a constant state of siege on residents. Together with the state's policies of economic and social marginalization, this repression is feeding the insurgency. This has shifted some sympathy from the military to the militants, who are increasingly seen as a way to take revenge. This has manifested itself in militants' shows of strength, including publicly evicting Coptic families from their homes in the city of al-Arish; the government was unable to stop the eviction process or, more startlingly, to return the refugees back to their homes. This indicates the central government's loss of control in Sinai, even though it has boasted of killing of thousands of militants and repeatedly proclaimed progress in fighting the insurgency. Moreover, based on local sources, the militants have started to impose control over the civilian population—for example by imposing taxes, enforcing wearing niqab, and raising tariffs on the smuggling tunnels in Rafah, where they live openly.

The combination of heavy repression, numerous civilian casualties, and the increased reliance on the use of airpower and heavy weaponry has not only alienated the local population, it has proven highly ineffective. The state could make its operations in Sinai more effective by collaborating with local tribes that have declared willingness to ally themselves with the Egyptian military. But, suspicious of the local tribes, the central government has been reluctant to arm them as part of its counterterrorism campaign. The Egyptian government's attachment to conventional warfare paradigms has failed to put down the insurgency, which has instead become emboldened to carry out a rising number of attacks.

Periodical and Internet Sources Biblography

The following articles have been selected to supplement the diverse views presented in this chapter.

Daniel Byman, "Why Drones Work: The Case for Washington's Weapon of Choice," *Foreign Affairs*, July/August 2013.

Amitai Etzioni, "The Great Drone Debate," *Military Review*, March/April 2013.

Ronald S. Friedman and Barbara Sutton, "Selling the War? System-Justifying Effects of Commercial Advertising on Civilian Casualty Tolerance," *Political Psychology*, June 2013.

Dr. Binoy Kampmark, "Warmongering and Necromancy: The US State Department Dissent on Syria," Counter Currents, June 21, 2016. http://www.countercurrents.org/2016/06/21/warmongering-and-necromancy-the-us-state-department-dissent-on-syria/.

Jared Keller, "The Futile War Against Civilian Casualties," *Pacific Standard*, June 5, 2017. https://psmag.com/social-justice/the-futile-war-against-civilian-casualties.

Jared Keller, "How the Pentagon Repurposes Civilian Casualties as Anti-Terror Propaganda," *Pacific Standard*, November 20, 2017. https://psmag.com/social-justice/how-the-pentagon-repurposes-civilian-casualties-as-anti-terror-propaganda.

Loveday Morris and Liz Sly, "Panic Spreads in Iraq, Syria as Record Numbers of Civilians Reported Killed in U.S. Strikes," *Chicago Tribune*, March 28, 2017. http://www.chicagotribune.com/news/nationworld/ct-islamic-state-airstrikes-iraq-syria-20170328-story.html.

William Neuman, "Colombia Military Accused of Deception on Civilian Deaths," *New York Times*, June 24, 2015. https://www.nytimes.com/2015/06/24/world/americas/colombia-military-accused-of-deception-on-civilian-deaths.html?_r=0.

Pressenza, "London Conference Decries Western Governments' Warmongering," February 10, 2013. https://www.pressenza.com/2013/02/london-conference-decries-western-governments-warmongering/.

Jon Rainwater, "Credo, Moveon.org, Peace Action, and Win without War Pledge to Resist Any Trump Administration Effort to

Propel the United States into a War of Choice," PeaceAction. org, March 29, 2017. https://www.peaceaction.org/2017/03/29/ credo-moveon-org-peace-action-and-win-without-war-pledge-to-resist-any-trump-administration-effort-to-propel-the-united-states-into-a-war-of-choice/.

Masud Wadan, "In Afghanistan, Civilian Deaths Happen by Design, Not by Accident," *Global Research*, May 20, 2017. https://www. globalresearch.ca/in-afghanistan-civilian-casualties-happen-by-design-not-by-accident/5590933.

Reed M. Wood and Jacob D. Kathman, "Competing for the Crown: Inter-rebel Competition and Civilian Targeting in Civil War," *Political Research Quarterly*, March 2015.

GLOBALVIEWPOINTS

CHAPTER 4

Protecting Against Civilian Casualties

The Geneva Conventions Protocols Protect Civilians

International Committee of the Red Cross

In the following viewpoint, the International Committee of the Red Cross presents the Geneva Conventions of 1949 and their additional protocols intended to protect those harmed during war. Of the four main conventions, only the Fourth Convention specifically addresses protection of civilians. Spurred by the aftermath of World War II, this set of 156 articles takes into consideration civilians in occupied territories. Common Article 3 supports all conventions and addresses civilian casualties in noninternational situations. Together, these conventions lay the foundation of international humanitarian law, and provide the means for prosecution of those who violate them. The International Committee of the Red Cross aids people affected by conflict and armed violence.

As you read, consider the following questions:

1. What is the purpose of the Fourth Geneva Convention?
2. What additional protections does Common Article 3 offer?
3. When did the Geneva Conventions become enforceable?

"The Geneva Conventions of 1949 and Their Additional Protocols," International Committee of the Red Cross, October 10, 2010. Reprinted by permission.

The 1949 Geneva Conventions

The first Geneva Convention protects wounded and sick soldiers on land during war. This Convention represents the fourth updated version of the Geneva Convention on the wounded and sick following those adopted in 1864, 1906 and 1929. It contains 64 articles. These provide protection for the wounded and sick, but also for medical and religious personnel, medical units and medical transports. The Convention also recognizes the distinctive emblems. It has two annexes containing a draft agreement relating to hospital zones and a model identity card for medical and religious personnel.

The second Geneva Convention protects wounded, sick and shipwrecked military personnel at sea during war. This Convention replaced Hague Convention of 1907 for the Adaptation to Maritime Warfare of the Principles of the Geneva Convention. It closely follows the provisions of the first Geneva Convention in structure and content. It has 63 articles specifically applicable to war at sea. For example, it protects hospital ships. It has one annex containing a model identity card for medical and religious personnel.

The third Geneva Convention applies to prisoners of war. This Convention replaced the Prisoners of War Convention of 1929. It contains 143 articles whereas the 1929 Convention had only 97. The categories of persons entitled to prisoner of war status were broadened in accordance with Conventions I and II. The conditions and places of captivity were more precisely defined, particularly with regard to the labour of prisoners of war, their financial resources, the relief they receive, and the judicial proceedings instituted against them. The Convention establishes the principle that prisoners of war shall be released and repatriated without delay after the cessation of active hostilities. The Convention has five annexes containing various model regulations and identity and other cards.

The fourth Geneva Convention affords protection to civilians, including in occupied territory. The Geneva Conventions, which were adopted before 1949, were concerned with combatants only, not with civilians. The events of World War II showed the disastrous consequences of the absence of a convention for the protection of civilians in wartime. The Convention adopted in 1949 takes account of the experiences of World War II. It is composed of 159 articles. It contains a short section concerning the general protection of populations against certain consequences of war, without addressing the conduct of hostilities, as such, which was later examined in the Additional Protocols of 1977. The bulk of the Convention deals with the status and treatment of protected persons, distinguishing between the situation of foreigners on the territory of one of the parties to the conflict and that of civilians in occupied territory. It spells out the obligations of the Occupying Power vis-à-vis the civilian population and contains detailed provisions on humanitarian relief for populations in occupied territory. It also contains a specific regime for the treatment of civilian internees. It has three annexes containing a model agreement on hospital and safety zones, model regulations on humanitarian relief and model cards.

Common Article 3

Article 3, common to the four Geneva Conventions, marked a breakthrough, as it covered, for the first time, situations of non-international armed conflicts. These types of conflicts vary greatly. They include traditional civil wars, internal armed conflicts that spill over into other States or internal conflicts in which third States or a multinational force intervenes alongside the government. Common Article 3 establishes fundamental rules from which no derogation is permitted. It is like a mini-Convention within the Conventions as it contains the essential rules of the Geneva Conventions in a condensed format and makes them applicable to conflicts not of an international character:

- It requires humane treatment for all persons in enemy hands, without any adverse distinction. It specifically prohibits murder, mutilation, torture, cruel, humiliating and degrading treatment, the taking of hostages and unfair trial.

- It requires that the wounded, sick and shipwrecked be collected and cared for.

- It grants the ICRC the right to offer its services to the parties to the conflict.

- It calls on the parties to the conflict to bring all or parts of the Geneva Conventions into force through so-called special agreements.

- It recognizes that the application of these rules does not affect the legal status of the parties to the conflict.

- Given that most armed conflicts today are non-international, applying Common Article 3 is of the utmost importance. Its full respect is required.

Where Do the Geneva Conventions Apply?

The Geneva Conventions entered into force on 21 October 1950.

Ratification grew steadily through the decades: 74 States ratified the Conventions during the 1950s, 48 States did so during the 1960s, 20 States signed on during the 1970s, and another 20 States did so during the 1980s. Twenty-six countries ratified the Conventions in the early 1990s, largely in the aftermath of the break-up of the Soviet Union, Czechoslovakia and the former Yugoslavia.

Seven new ratifications since 2000 have brought the total number of States Party to 194, making the Geneva Conventions universally applicable.

The Additional Protocols to the Geneva Conventions

In the two decades that followed the adoption of the Geneva Conventions, the world witnessed an increase in the number of non-international armed conflicts and wars of national liberation. In response, two Protocols Additional to the four 1949 Geneva Conventions were adopted in 1977. They strengthen the protection of victims of international (Protocol I) and non-international

(Protocol II) armed conflicts and place limits on the way wars are fought. Protocol II was the first-ever international treaty devoted exclusively to situations of non-international armed conflicts.

In 2005, a third Additional Protocol was adopted creating an additional emblem, the Red Crystal, which has the same international status as the Red Cross and Red Crescent emblems.

In Europe, War Has Long-Term Effects on Health and Economic Status

Iris Kesternich, Bettina Siflinger, James P. Smith, and Joachim K. Winter

In the following excerpted viewpoint, international economics scholars contend that World War II provides a natural environment for studying the effects of war. Their study reveals that those exposed to war experience greater probability of developing diabetes, depression, and other health issues, especially among members of the middle class. Kesternich is Associate Professor, Department of Economics, University of Leuven, Belgium. Siflinger is Assistant Professor, Department of Econometrics and Operations Research, Tiburg University, Netherlands. Smith is Distinguished Chair, Labor Markets and Demographic Studies, RAND Corporation, US. Winter is Chair, Department of Empirical Economic Research, University of Munich, Germany.

As you read, consider the following questions:

1. Why does World War II present opportunities for European economic research?
2. Where did most of the study's data come from?
3. Who does this study suggest has been more affected by war?

"The Effects of World War II on Economic and Health Outcomes across Europe," by Iris Kesternich, Bettina Siflinger, James P. Smith, and Joachim K. Winter, President and Fellows of Harvard College and the Massachusetts Institute of Technology, volume 96, issue 1, (March 2014): pp. 103–118. Reprinted by permission of MIT Press Journals.

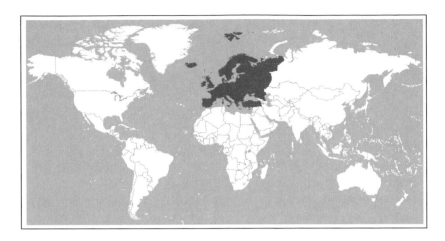

The Second World War (WWII) was one of the major transformative events of the 20th century, with 39 million deaths in Europe alone. Large amounts of physical capital were destroyed through six years of ground battles and bombing. Many individuals were forced to abandon or give up their property without compensation and to move on to new lands. Periods of hunger became more common even in relatively prosperous Western Europe. Families were separated for long periods of time, and many children lost their fathers. Many, including young children, would personally witness the horrors of war as battles and bombing took place in the very areas where they lived. Horrendous crimes against humanity were committed. Due to WWII, political and economic systems in many countries would be permanently altered.

In this paper, we investigate long-run effects of World War II on late-life economic and health outcomes in Western continental Europe (health, education, labor market outcomes and marriage). We explore several channels through which this war might have influenced individual lives, and document which groups of the population were most affected. Our research relies on retrospective life data from the European Survey of Health, Aging, and Retirement in Europe (SHARE) that have recently become available. SHARE covers representative samples of the population aged 50 and over in 13 European countries, with about 20,000 observations. We also collected external data on casualties, timing and location of combat action, yearly GDP by country, population movements, and male-female population ratios. To our individual-level analysis of the multidimensional effects of a major shock that affected life circumstances, we add new dimensions to a rapidly increasing literature that aims at explaining the causes of health and wealth gradients in labor and health economics (see Deaton, 2007; Smith, 2009a; Heckman, 2012).

SHARE not only measures major contemporaneous economic and health outcomes of adults over age 50 in these European countries, but includes retrospective modules meant to capture salient parts of early life experiences, including those related to the war. There simply are no micro economic panel data in either the United States or in Europe that have prospectively tracked people for that long a time period. The co-existence of current prospective data combined with retrospective data on key events that preceded the survey baseline opens up important new research opportunities not before possible, and not simply those associated with the WWII. Since the end of WWII, western continental Europe has had a rich and sometime tumultuous economic and political history, the effects of which on its residents are not well documented.

There is legitimate concern about the quality of recall data, particularly for time periods decades in the past. But that concern has been lessened by a realization that recall of events during childhood is better than for other periods of life, particularly if events are salient as they certainly are in this application. Smith (2009b) investigated several quality markers and showed that his childhood health instrument was successful in matching known secular trends in childhood illnesses decades in the past. Moreover, we will provide evidence in this paper that these recalled events in the SHARE retrospective about the war matched the historical record.

One aim of the paper is to illustrate how such retrospective life data can further our understanding of effects of early-life conditions as affected by large external shocks, such as a war. The existing literature measuring impacts of macro-events mostly used "natural experiments" such as wars or famines to study effects of early-life conditions at the aggregate level. Largely due to data reasons beyond their control, the studies of which we are aware could not use individual-level measures of whether a particular person was affected by the war and through which channel. Retrospective life data, such as those from SHARE, contain detailed information and provide the opportunity of studying that issue.

Analyzing different outcomes is a first step in understanding the channels and mechanisms by which wars affect people's lives. Another possibility is using different measures of war exposure such as the closeness of combat. We construct such measures from external data sources. In addition, SHARE data contain retrospective questions on several possible channels of war exposure: hunger, the absence of the father, dispossession, and persecution.

Given the scale of the war and number of ways it fundamentally changed the world, the existing economic literature using WWII as a natural experiment is surprisingly thin. Moreover, the literature that does exist using WWII is relatively recent and more American in context than European. This may reflect the fact that the popularity of "natural experiments" framework in economics itself post-dated WWII by many decades. Still, it does suggest that excellent research opportunities remain, especially given the wide diversity of European experiences in WWII.

[...]

To conduct this analysis we use new data—SHARELIFE— that records not only adult outcomes in 2009, but also contains retrospective data for salient aspects of the wartime experiences of respondents. We augment these data with historical information on how WWII affected individuals differently over time and across regions. Our data allow us to analyze which type of individuals were most affected, and by which channels.

Our analysis shows that experiencing war increased the probability of suffering from diabetes, depression, and with less certainty heart disease so that those experiencing war or combat have significantly lower self-rated health as adults. Experiencing war is also associated with less education and life satisfaction, and decreases the probability of ever being married for women, while increasing it for men. We also analyze pathways through which these wartime effects took place and found strong effects for hunger, dispossession, persecution, childhood immunizations, and having an absent father. While a war of the magnitude of WWII affected all social classes to some degree, our evidence does suggest that the more severe effects were on the middle class with the lower class right below them in size of impact.

This paper highlights advantages of having life-histories in prospective studies such as SHARE. Population-based economic panels are relatively recent, but combining them with life-histories covering salient past personal and macro events opens up many new research opportunities of which WWII is only one illustration. This is especially so in Western Europe where the political and economic history of the past four decades is particularly rich and varied.

Protecting Civilians Is a Peacekeeping Priority for the United Nations

Citizens for Global Solutions

In the following viewpoint, Citizens for Global Solutions argues that many factors challenge peacekeepers in protecting civilians. Complex factors affect the ability of civilian and military peacekeepers, including planning and implementation, geographic scope, and security. Without civilian protections, peacekeeping and relief organizations cannot do their jobs effectively or efficiently. One such organization is the UN Security Council, which passed important resolutions such as 2006's Resolution 1674 that makes clear it will honor the commitment to protect civilians in armed conflict. Citizens for Global Solutions works to build political will in the United States for international cooperation and democratic global institutions that establish peace, justice, and sustainability under the rule of law.

As you read, consider the following questions:

1. Why is the safety of civilians important to peacekeeping organizations?
2. What is the role of the UN Security Council with respect to civilian protection?
3. From a humanitarian view, civilian protection means providing humanitarian assistance and guaranteeing a standard of human rights. What does civilian protection mean to the military?

"Protecting Civilians in Armed Conflict," Citizens for Global Solutions. Reprinted by permission.

I n contemporary armed conflicts, innocent civilians often constitute an overwhelming majority of victims and have at times been deliberately targeted. The most vulnerable populations at risk include women and children, who are often killed, raped and sexually abused, kidnapped and enslaved, and children, who are taken and forced to become soldiers. Survivors are often displaced, by force or for lack of choice, taking refuge in camps where they are often defenseless against armed attacks and harassment. Many are maimed by mines and other indiscriminate munitions. Even more die of the indirect effects of armed conflict: disease, malnutrition, and famine.

What Is Civilian Protection?

Protecting civilians has emerged as a central purpose of many contemporary peace operations. Both civilian and military peacekeepers increasingly recognize the moral duty and operational importance of protecting threatened civilian populations during peacekeeping operations. As peacekeeping missions have grown in number, frequency, size and mandate, the UN has made increasingly concerted efforts to put civilian protection at the heart of these operations. How well peacekeeping missions protect civilians is often an important benchmark for evaluating a mission's effectiveness.

There are legal, political, and operational aspects of protecting civilians as well as accompanying challenges. Protecting civilians is a complex process involving many different actors (international, regional, and local stakeholders) over time (from planning into execution). The challenges to civilian protection are vast, ranging from the scale of the needs on the ground and the challenging security environment, to the lack of infrastructure. Often, lack of operational clarity hampers the ability of UN peacekeepers to protect civilians that suffer the effects of armed conflict. Peacekeepers are often responsible for protecting large populations spread over vast territories, but they usually lack personnel and material resources to do so effectively, such as a deficiency of resources like helicopters, which allow them to access remote areas relatively quickly.

Why Civilian Protection Matters

Consensus is forming around the importance of protecting civilians not only because of the humanitarian obligation to shelter endangered populations from the effects of armed conflict. Overall, civilian protection is essential because it is critical to the perceived success of peacekeeping operations and therefore the UN's ability to work credibly in the field of peace and security.

Many groups deliberately target civilians as a tactic to achieve their political goals, including government forces, armed rebel groups, and terrorist organizations. The security of the population is also a prerequisite for an enduring political arrangement between two warring groups. Thus civilian protection is important to the broader political goals of creating and upholding peace agreements. Preventing attacks on civilians also preempts spoilers from creating instability and weakening fragile peace processes in post-war environments.

Moreover, humanitarian assistance cannot be provided by relief agencies, international and regional organizations, and NGOs when civilians and third party providers are at risk of being attacked. The security of civilians is also a key aspect of providing development assistance in post-conflict situations.

The United Nations and the Civilian Protection Agenda

The Security Council has set important precedents for civilian protection through its statements, resolutions, and perhaps most importantly, the mandates of UN peace operations. The first of these landmark resolutions was in 1999, when the Security Council unanimously voted in favor of Resolution 1265, which addressed the Council's inclination to take "appropriate measures" in response to situations where civilians are being targeted or humanitarian assistance is deliberately circumvented. The resolution also called on states to hold leaders accountable for acts of genocide, crimes against humanity and other serious violations of international humanitarian law. The most important precedent resulting from the resolution was a willingness to consider expanding the peacekeeping mandate to better protect civilian populations. Shortly afterward, it became unofficial UN policy that when peacekeepers saw violence perpetrated against civilians, they should be "presumed to be authorized to stop it, within their means." This is a point of controversy because it invokes Chapter VII of the UN Charter—the clause that governs the use of force— but it also affects a peacekeeping mission's ability to act impartially.

In 2006, the Security Council passed Resolution 1674, committing it to take action to protect civilians in armed conflict. The UN also has set civilian protection precedents in the mandates of specific missions, including the Democratic Republic of Congo (MONUC/MONUSCO), Sudan (UNAMID and UNMIS), and Afghanistan (ACRO). Over time, the emphasis on civilian protection has increased and become a frequent staple for UN peace operations.

Other UN organs and agencies, in particular the General Assembly Special Committee on Peacekeeping (known as the C34), the Department of Peacekeeping Operations, and the Office for the Coordination of Humanitarian Affairs, have included the topic of civilian protection in their agendas and enhanced their efforts to protect endangered civilian populations. For example, the C34 recently released a report requesting UN peace operations to design specific and comprehensive strategies for civilian protection through integrated planning to ensure the prioritization of civilian protection in the overall mission strategy. Moreover, the creation of the position of Deputy Special Representative for the Secretary General for Humanitarian Affairs has improved the coordination of civilian protection efforts among UN agencies as well as with the relevant NGOs on the ground.

Killer Robots Could Minimize Casualties of Innocent Noncombatants

Let me unequivocally state: The status quo with respect to innocent civilian casualties is utterly and wholly unacceptable. I am not Pro Lethal Autonomous Weapon Systems (LAWS), nor for lethal weapons of any sort. I would hope that LAWS would never need to be used, as I am against killing in all its manifold forms. But if humanity persists in entering into warfare, which is an unfortunate underlying assumption, we must protect the innocent noncombatants in the battlespace far better than we currently do. Technology can, must, and should be used toward that end. Is it not our responsibility as scientists to look for effective ways to reduce man's inhumanity to man through technology? Research in ethical military robotics could and should be applied toward achieving this goal.

I have studied ethology (animal behavior in their natural environment) as a basis for robotics for my entire career, spanning frogs, insects, dogs, birds, wolves, and human companions. Nowhere has it been more depressing than to study human behavior in the battlefield (for example, the Surgeon General's Office 2006 report and Killing Civilians: Method, Madness, and Morality in War.). The commonplace occurrence of slaughtering civilians in conflict over millennia gives rise to my pessimism in reforming human behavior yet provides optimism for robots being able to exceed human moral performance in similar circumstances. The regular commission of atrocities is well documented both historically and in the present day, reported almost on a daily basis. Due to this unfortunate low bar, my claim that robots may be able to eventually outperform humans with respect to adherence to international humanitarian law (IHL) in warfare (that is, be more humane) is credible. I have the utmost respect for our young men and women in the battlespace, but they are placed into situations where no human has ever been designed to function. This is exacerbated by the tempo at which modern warfare is conducted. Expecting widespread compliance with IHL given this pace and resultant stress seems unreasonable and perhaps unattainable by flesh and blood warfighters.

"The Case for Banning Killer Robots: Counterpoint," by Ronald Arkin, The Association for Computing Machinery.

Conceptual Developments and Operational Innovations

One of the most essential conceptual innovations in the area of civilian protection has been the establishment and popularization of the responsibility to protect (R2P). The international community's failure to protect civilians and prevent genocide in the 1990's resulted in the recognition of the need to address the specific vulnerabilities of civilian populations. A new international norm emerged: the responsibility to protect (R2P). One of three pillars of the concept of R2P is the international responsibility to respond effectively through the UN when governments are "manifestly failing" to protect their populations from any of the four crimes under international humanitarian law: war crimes, crimes against humanity, ethnic cleansing, and genocide. While the concept has its origins in theory and academia, it has gained widespread recognition and popularity as a foundational approach to address the terrible crimes that are perpetrated against civilians—during war but also in peace time. The UN has even appointed a special advisor on the issue and in 2007, the new Secretary-General Ban Ki-moon prioritized making R2P a reality.

Civilian protection and R2P are based on the same underlying principles, but they remain distinct. In essence, R2P focuses on preventing and stopping the most horrendous crimes (genocide, ethnic cleansing, war crimes and crimes against humanity) whether they occur within the context of armed conflicts or not. The concept of civilian protection focuses on the broader list of specific threats, vulnerabilities and needs of civilian populations in armed conflicts, from physical security to food security and other humanitarian needs.

Operational innovations in civilian protection include practical steps taken by various actors to create specific guidance on civilian protection and highlight best practices. On the ground, several missions—primarily MONUC (now MONUSCO) in the Democratic Republic of Congo and UNAMID in Darfur—have spearheaded practical innovations to enhance civilian protection despite limited resources and difficult environments. These operations have increasingly used and developed mobile operational bases, quick responses units, and early-warning systems to anticipate, prevent, deter or rapidly intervene to stop violence against civilians.

Joint protection teams and protection clusters have enhanced the effectiveness of these efforts by providing a more comprehensive approach to civilian protection to include humanitarian relief as well as social and economic support to threatened civilian populations. It also targets the perpetrators of violence through deterrence, supports disarmament and reintegration of former combatants and fosters reconciliation on the ground to ensure sustainable security for civilian populations.

Challenges and Next Steps: The Future of Civilian Protection

Numerous challenges and shortcomings impede the capacity of peacekeepers to effectively protect civilians on the ground. As UN Secretary-General Ban Ki-moon recently acknowledged, the relevant actors continue to struggle over what it means for peacekeeping operations to protect civilians, in both definition and practice. The perennial problem of many operations is summarized best by the Brahimi Report from 2000: peacekeepers may not be able to justifiably use force against attackers in order to protect civilians when they feel "morally compelled" to do so. Despite developments in peacekeeping mission mandates, it is not always clear how these mandates translate into operations on a case by case basis, creating situations wherein troops and police are not clear on what is expected of them. As a result, there is a lack of cohesion between mandates, intentions, and expectations, especially if civilian protection requires the use of force.

A continuing challenge is the division between human rights and humanitarian organizations that envision civilian protection being a broader concept that includes humanitarian assistance and guarantees of human rights standards, whereas militarily-oriented institutions see protection as preventing physical harm. So far, the official guidelines from the UN provide little detail on what defines civilian protection.

In the future, the greatest challenge will be how peacekeepers can deter attacks on civilians. Continuing to maintain relations with host countries is also going to be an important issue in the coming years. For example, how can civilians be protected when the host government bans peacekeepers from entering the country, or if a host government decides to expel peacekeepers before they have completed their mandates? It will also be essential to future missions to be able to reflect on past successes and failures. For future missions, it will be increasingly crucial for information to be gathered from current missions in order to evaluate, analyze, and contextualize their work on civilian protection.

Finally, there is a need to match peacekeepers' protection mandates with appropriate resources, including providing specific training on civilian protection, developing civilian protection doctrines and practical guidance, as well as fostering international political support—especially within the Security Council.

In Yemen, Bridges and Hospitals as Civilian Objects Must Be Spared Military Targeting

Beth Van Schaack

In the following excerpted viewpoint, Beth Van Schaack maintains that international humanitarian law can and should be applied to any armed conflict incident. She evaluates the Saudi-led coalition attack on a bridge in Yemen, a place on the US's "no strike" list. She also analyzes a Saudi attack on a Doctors Without Borders hospital. She argues that the attacks could have been prevented had the attackers kept the concept of proportionality, that is, minimizing the potential number of civilian casualties, in mind. She also argues that bridges and hospitals should be considered non-military objects and should therefore not be targeted.

As you read, consider the following questions:

1. Where can key concepts for evaluating the legality of the Yemeni bridge incident be found?
2. Why did the US include the Yemeni bridge on its "no strike" list?
3. Why should bridges and hospitals be considered civilian objects? How should international humanitarian law protect them?

"Evaluating Proportionality and Long-Term Civilian Harm under the Laws of War," by Beth Van Schaack, Just Security, August 29, 2016. Reprinted by permission.

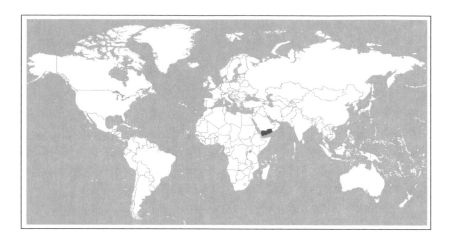

The law of armed conflict, or international humanitarian law (IHL), contains broad principles and prohibitions that are applied to a set of concrete facts in the context of any armed conflict. This analysis happens both ex ante—as a target set is being identified and an attack is launched—and ex post—when a completed operation is being evaluated for its compliance with IHL, including the war crimes prohibitions.

The Saudi-led coalition's August 11 attack on a bridge in Yemen helps to exemplify the difficulty in applying these concepts to real-world examples. The details of the attack remain rather sparse (some of the best reporting on this topic is here). What we do know is that the bridge in question was located on the main road from the port city of Hodeidah to the capital of Sanaa. In addition, we know, and presumably the attackers also knew, that an enormous amount (90% to be exact) of the food coming from the U.N. World Food Program and other humanitarian actors apparently traversed that bridge en route to civilians in need. This food aid is helping to keep the Yemeni civilian population alive: over half of the country's population (14 million souls) are suffering from malnutrition and food insecurity. According to UNICEF, more than 300,000 children under the age of 5 have acute malnutrition, which can lead to death and long-term developmental, cognitive, and other impairments. It's been reported that the United States considered the bridge to be a piece of vital infrastructure and thus included it on a "no strike" list. The State Department has accordingly denounced the attack:

> We have seen those reports, and if the bridge was deliberately struck by coalition forces, we would find this completely unacceptable. The bridge was critical for the delivery, as you note, for humanitarian assistance. Destruction will further complicate efforts to provide assistance to the people of Yemen.

The spokesperson later clarified that her statement was meant to be a "condemnation"—strong language when it comes to international diplomacy. At the same time, she also rebuked the most recent (of many) Saudi attack on a Médecins sans Frontières hospital. The International Committee of the Red Cross and Amnesty International, among others, have blamed Saudi Arabia for deliberately targeting hospitals and medical facilities since that country first overtly intervened in the conflict in March 2015.

This post walks through the analysis necessary to evaluate the attack on the bridge and concludes that the attack in question should have been precluded had the attackers respected the principle of proportionality in light of the facts as we know them. The post concludes with a quick discussion of the potential war crimes that could be charged depending on the facts that emerge and other legal implications of the attack.

International Humanitarian Law Principles

The key concepts for evaluating the legality of the destruction of the bridge are found in Additional Protocol I to the four Geneva Conventions of 1949. Unlike its "parent" treaties, API has not yet achieved universal ratification (there are 174 members at present, including Saudi Arabia), but many of its terms are considered to be part of customary international law (CIL) by the International Committee of the Red Cross (ICRC), states parties, and even non-party states. Although API by its terms applies to international armed conflicts, many the most important rules apply across the conflict spectrum by way of CIL and appear in other IHL treaties addressed to non-international armed conflicts (NIACs),

Prioritizing Civilian Protection in Syria and Iraq

As the United States undertakes a more robust role in the fight against the Islamic State of Iraq and Syria (ISIS), Center for Civilians in Conflict (CIVIC) is concerned about the potential for considerable civilian harm. It is imperative that planning for military operations and the training and equipping of Syrian rebel groups include practical measures to minimize civilian harm.

"In attacks against ISIS, it's vital that the US apply the lessons already learned in Iraq and Afghanistan about avoiding harm to civilians, and responding effectively when harm does occur," said Marla Keenan, managing director of CIVIC. "Avoiding harm to civilians, and having policies for meaningful responses to causalities, are absolutely critical to any military success," Keenan said. "Making civilian protection a priority is as important a part of a strategy as the choice of military targets. If civilians are not protected, and if harm to them is not promptly recognized, any military success can be quickly undone."

Some air and naval operations are directing fire at populated areas. While US officials have spoken about the need to avoid civilian casualties, it is mission critical to ensure policies and practices are in place to assess the impact of all operations on civilians.

Practical tools, tactical guidance, and assessments on civilian casualties undertaken by the US and international forces in Afghanistan are instructive on how military operations in Syria and Iraq should be conducted to ensure civilian harm is minimized. Specifically, the US should:

- Ensure intelligence feeding into targeting decisions is sufficiently vetted and includes information on civilians in proximity to improve accuracy;
- Perform rigorous collateral damage estimates (CDEs) before strikes and battle damage assessments (BDAs) afterwards;
- Create a "Civilian Casualty Tracking Cell"—a database and staff focused on aggregating and analyzing the information from CDEs and BDAs to provide information on if and how civilians are being harmed so commanders can adjust tactics and techniques to better avoid civilian harm; and,
- Create the capacity to appropriately respond to any alleged civilian harm including investigations and the making of appropriate amends to victims.

"US: Civilian Protection Should be Prioritized in Syria and Iraq Operations," by Christopher Allbritton, Center for Civilians in Conflict, September 25, 2014.

like the one in Yemen. For example, the Convention on Certain Conventional Weapons and its Protocols embody verbatim many of the same targeting rules as contained in API.

The Principle of Distinction

The principle of distinction is foundational to IHL. As applied to objects, this principle dictates that:

> The parties to the conflict must at all times distinguish between civilian objects and military objectives. Attacks may only be directed against military objectives. Attacks must not be directed against civilian objects.

The first question is thus: was the bridge a military objective? If not, then the attack is per se unlawful (unless it could be shown to be truly accidental, which was clearly not the case here). Even if the bridge can be characterized as a military objective, the attack on it may still be unlawful if any collateral damage to the civilian population was disproportionate to the military advantage to be gained.

Military Objectives v. Civilian Objects

The definition of "military objective," as set forth in Article 52(2) of API, is generally cited as definitive. (Note, however, that there is some lingering debate about whether the definition is broad enough to cover war-sustaining objects as discussed in greater detail in Ryan Goodman's new paper as well as my and Kenneth Watkin's analyses on these pages). The standard definition of military objective reads:

> Attacks shall be limited strictly to military objectives. In so far as objects are concerned, military objectives are limited to those objects which
> - by their nature, location, purpose or use make an effective contribution to military action and
> - whose partial or total destruction, capture or neutralization, in the circumstances ruling at the time, offers a definite military advantage.

This definition contains two prongs addressed to two sets of actors: the attacker and the defender. The desired target must make an effective contribution to the military action of the defender (by its nature, location, purpose or use); and its destruction, capture, or neutralization must offer a definite military advantage to the attacker. In practice, these two prongs tend to collapse into each other given that it is difficult to imagine one prong being satisfied without the other.

In terms of the first prong, the proposed target must make an "effective" contribution to military action, but not necessarily a "direct" one. An impact could thus be indirect but still effective. The term "military action" is not defined, but is clearly broader than the concept of a "military operation." A particular target can offer a military advantage that is felt over a lengthy period of time; it can also affect military action in areas other than in its immediate vicinity. At the same time, it is not entirely clear how far removed from military activities the object's contribution can be to still qualify as a military objective susceptible to direct attack.

A feature like a bridge can be a military objective by means of its location, use, or purpose. "Purpose" is often conceived of as "intended future use" in contradistinction to "use," which implies current utility. The difficulty of knowing, at the time target sets are being drawn up, the intended future use of some objects without extremely granular intelligence should not be underestimated. Targeting a civilian object because it might potentially make an effective contribution to military action at some future date is obviously problematic. Theoretically, every civilian object could—at some point in time and under some circumstance or another—be used for military action. Rendering such objects universally targetable on the basis of a commander's ability to articulate some future military use would vitiate the principle of distinction altogether.

In terms of the second prong of the definition, the advantage gained to the attacker in destroying the proposed target must be substantial and relatively proximate rather than hypothetical, speculative, or distal. It is often stated that the military advantage can be evaluated by the attack as a whole and not necessarily isolated components of it, although how far this reaches remains somewhat controversial.

IHL treaties and articulations of CIL contain a presumption of civilian status that applies both to persons and things. In cases of doubt about how to classify and object or potential target, it shall be presumed that it is not being used to make an effective contribution to military action. The US Department of Defense has taken the position that this presumption is not part of CIL, however, because such a rule would shift the burden of determining the precise use of an object from the defender to the attacker (i.e., to a party that does not exercise control over the object). Specifically, the Department of Defense's Law of War Manual at §5.5.3.2 states:

> Under customary international law, no legal presumption of civilian status exists for persons or objects, nor is there any rule inhibiting commanders or other military personnel from acting based on the information available to him or her in doubtful cases.

Although there is no definitive list of legitimate military objectives, categorical examples include weapons caches, barracks, and military transports. Conversely, places of worship, schools, museums, monuments, and hospitals—so long as they have not lost their civilian character by being employed in military action— are considered civilian objects. The ICRC lists "civilian means of transportation" as an example of "prima facie civilian object[s]."

Back to the bridge: From the facts available in open-source accounts, it does not appear that the Houthi rebels were using the bridge for military action at the time it was attacked. That said, hindering an opponent's ability to transport material, armaments, or personnel; fragmenting an adversary by isolating units from each other and command and control apparatus; and cutting off transportation routes would clearly offer the attacker an advantage. Indeed, the DoD's Law of War Manual at

§5.7.7.3 uses the destruction of a bridge to exemplify the concept of military objective:

> the military advantage in the attack of an individual bridge may not be seen immediately (particularly if, at the time of the attack, there is no military traffic in the area), but can be established by the overall effort to isolate enemy military forces on the battlefield through the destruction of bridges.

> [...]

The principle of proportionality dictates that:

> Launching an attack which may be expected to cause incidental loss of civilian life, injury to civilians, damage to civilian objects, or a combination thereof, which would be excessive in relation to the concrete and direct military advantage anticipated, is prohibited.

> [...]

In order to be in compliance with these obligations, warring parties are required to take "all" feasible precautions to minimize civilian harm. According to the ICRC's CIL Study:

> Each party to the conflict must take all feasible precautions in the choice of means and methods of warfare with a view to avoiding, and in any event to minimizing, incidental loss of civilian life, injury to civilians and damage to civilian objects.

In this regard, states must make affirmative efforts to protect the civilian population from the effects of attacks.

A range of precautions are available to belligerents, including target verification exercises, considerations about the timing of an attack, avoiding populated areas, warning civilians co-located with military objectives, incapacitating versus destroying particular objectives, and selecting precise weapons and weapon systems. When a choice is possible between several military objectives that would result in the same military advantage, "the objective to be selected must be that [which] may be expected to cause the least danger to civilian lives and to civilian objects."

Periodical and Internet Sources Bibliography

The following articles have been selected to supplement the diverse views presented in this chapter.

Lisa Hultman, Jacob Kathman, and Megan Shannon, "United Nations Peacekeeping and Civilian Protection in Civil War," *American Journal of Political Science*, October 2013.

International Committee of the Red Cross, "Protection of Civilians in Armed Conflict," May 25, 2017. https://www.icrc.org/en/document/protection-civilians-armed-conflict.

International Justice Resource Center, "UN Reports Civilian Casualties, Rights Abuses Remain High in Afghanistan," July 24, 2017. http://www.ijrcenter.org/2017/07/24/un-reports-civilian-casualties-rights-abuses-remain-high-in-afghanistan/.

Oliver Kaplan, "Protecting Civilians in Civil War: The Institution of the ATCC in Colombia," *Journal of Peace Research*, May 2013.

Andrew H. Kydd and Scott Straus, "The Road to Hell? Third-Party Intervention to Prevent Atrocities," *American Journal of Political Science*, July 2013.

Harry Lewis and Sarah Holewinski, "Changing of the Guard: Civilian Protection for an Evolving Military," *Prism*, March 2013.

Nate Moir, "The Civilian Casualties Management Team: A Piece of the Counterinsurgency Puzzle," Global Ecco. https://globalecco.org/the-civilian-casualties-management-team-a-piece-of-the-counterinsurgency-puzzle.

Sahr Muhammedally, "Minimizing Civilian Harm in Populated Areas," *International Review of the Red Cross*, April 2016.

Andy Oppenheimer, "Blast Simulation: Protecting Lives from IEDs," *Military Technology*, 2014.

United States Army Combined Arms Center, "Civilian Casualty (CIVCAS) Prevention GTA 90-01-039," May 2016. http://usacac.army.mil/organizations/mccoe/call/news/GTA_90_01_039.

White House Office of the Press Secretary, "Executive Order: United States Policy on Pre- and Post-Strike Measures to Address Civilian Casualties in U.S. Operations Involving the Use of Force," July 1, 2016. https://obamawhitehouse.archives.gov/the-press-office/2016/07/01/executive-order-united-states-policy-pre-and-post-strike-measures.

For Further Discussion

Chapter 1

1. Why are civilian deaths difficult to record and estimate? How does this affect policies and strategies of governments and their militaries?
2. Why are civilian deaths—specifically deaths of children—increasing in the fight against ISIS? Can anything be done to change this?

Chapter 2

1. Should the leaders in the War on Terror be held accountable for their actions as the World War II leaders were? Why or why not?
2. Do you think programs like the Foreign Claims Act are intended to be genuine or are they a political move to gain civilian support for war? Provide details to support your answer.

Chapter 3

1. How has war changed in the past few decades, and how has fighting of the "new wars" affected civilian casualties?
2. Can militaries ever go back to the "old" way of fighting, when civilian deaths were less frequent?

Chapter 4

1. Are the Geneva Conventions still relevant? Why or why not?
2. What is the responsibility of the international community when it comes to curbing civilian casualties? What strategies can be implemented to achieve this?

Organizations to Contact

The editors have compiled the following list of organizations concerned with the issues debated in this book. The descriptions are derived from materials provided by the organizations. All have publications or information available for interested readers. The list was compiled on the date of publication of the present volume; the information provided here may change. Be aware that many organizations take several weeks or longer to respond to inquiries, so allow as much time as possible.

Airwars
+44 (0)207 296 4242
email: info@airwars.org
website: www.airwars.org

Airwars is a nonprofit project based in the United Kingdom. It tracks and maintains information and statistics about air strikes against ISIS and other groups in Libya, Iraq, and Syria. It prides itself on providing reliable data and analysis. It is one of the sources for the numbers of civilian casualties.

American Civil Liberties Union
125 Broad Street, 18th floor
New York, NY 10004
(212) 549-2500
website: www.aclu.org

The American Civil Liberties Union, established nearly 100 years ago, works to safeguard each American's rights guaranteed under the US Constitution. It has more than 2 million members and fights against injustices in all 50 states, Puerto Rico, and Washington, DC. It has a reputation for tackling the toughest challenges to defend and maintain people's rights.

Amnesty International

1 Easton Street
London WC1X 0DW
United Kingdom
+44 20 7413 5500
website: www.amnesty.org

Amnesty International, a worldwide movement of more than 7 million people, dedicates itself to fighting against injustice and advocating for human rights. It works to ensure powerful groups keep their promises. In 2002, after a nine-year struggle, it established an International Criminal Court to hold accountable people responsible for war crimes and genocides.

The Brookings Institution

1775 Massachusetts Avenue NW
Washington, DC 20036
(202) 797-6000
website: www.brookings.edu

The Brookings Institution is a nonprofit public policy organization. By bringing together more than 300 well-known experts from around the world, it conducts research that recommends innovative solutions to public policy issues, including civilian casualties.

Center for Civil Society and Democracy

email: info@ccsd.ngo
website: www.ccsd.ngo

The Center for Civil Society and Democracy was established in 2012. It is an independent, nonprofit, nongovernmental organization (NGO). Its mission is to ensure a society where human rights and basic freedoms reign supreme. It operates in seven countries: Jordan, Lebanon, the Netherlands, Northern Iraq, Syria, Turkey, and the United States.

Center for Civilians in Conflict
1850 M Street NW, Suite 350
Washington, DC 20036
(202) 558-6958
email: info@civiliansinconflict.org
website: civiliansinconflict.org/

The Center for Civilians in Conflict works as an advocate for civilians caught in conflict. It develops and implements solutions to prevent and reduce harm caused to civilians. Part of that work also involves protecting civilians caught in conflict.

Hoover Institution
434 Galvez Mall
Stanford University
Stanford, CA 94305-6003
(650) 723-1754
website: www.hoover.org

The Hoover Institution pulls together its renowned scholars, library, and archives to improve the human condition. It recommends ideas that advocate for improved economic opportunity and prosperity. The organization is more than fifty years old and also has an office in Washington, DC.

Human Rights Watch
350 Fifth Avenue, 34th floor
New York, NY 10118-3299
(212) 290-4700
website: www.hrw.org

Human Rights Watch is a nonprofit organization with about 400 staff members around the world. It was established in 1978 and is known for presenting facts and objective reporting. It publishes a number of reports in its advocacy to protect and fight for human rights and justice. Staff members include lawyers, journalists, professors, and country-specific subject matter experts.

International Committee of the Red Cross
19 Avenue de la paix
1202 Geneva
Switzerland
+41 22 734 60 01
website: www.icrc.org

The International Committee of the Red Cross adheres to the Geneva Conventions of 1949 and additional protocols and statutes. It is an independent organization working to ensure humanitarian protection and help for armed conflict victims. It responds to emergencies. It also upholds international humanitarian law and promotes its proper implementation in national courts.

International Justice Resource Center
5 3rd Street, Suite 707
San Francisco, VA 94103
(415) 735-4180
email: ijrc@ijrcenter.org
website: www.ijrcenter.org

The International Justice Resource Center helps victims of human rights violations and civil society organizations with resources they can use for legal protection before international and their own country's courts. It provides education and training as well as advice to individuals and groups globally.

Organization for Security & Co-operation in Europe (OSCE)
Wallnerstrasse 6
1010 Vienna
Austria
+43 1 514 360
website: www.osce.org

The OSCE works to ensure politico-military, economic, environment, and human security across its 57 participating states in Europe, North America, and Central Asia. Among its many initiatives, it fights to counter terrorism and to advocate for human rights, keeping national minorities safe. It offers many documents and publications that target hate crime.

Organization for World Peace
website: www.theowp.org

The Organization for World Peace searches for peaceful solutions to war, international security, and destruction. It helps those affected by conflict. It also conducts and publishes research to further its cause of using noncombative methods to resolve conflicts. The OWP has offices in North America, Africa, Europe, Australia, and New Zealand.

Peace Action
2201 Broadway, Suite 321
Oakland, CA 94612
(800) 949-9020
8630 Fenton Street, Suite 524
Silver Spring, MD 20910
(301) 565-4050
website: www.peaceaction.org

Peace Action is a large grassroots organization in America that believes every person deserves the right to be free from violence and war. It works with members of Congress to develop US foreign policy that promotes peace, democracy, and human rights versus mass destruction. It was established in 1957 and has offices in both California and Maryland.

United Nations Refugee Agency
Case Postale 2500
VH-1211 Genève 2 Dépôt
Switzerland
+41 22 739 8111
www.unhcr.org

The United Nations Refugee Agency works globally to protect the rights of and provide a future for refugees, displaced communities, and people forced out of their countries. It also dedicates itself to saving lives.

World Health Organization
+41 22 791 2222
email: mediainquiries@who.int
website: www.who.int

The World Health Organization was established in 1948 and is headquartered in Geneva. Its staff consists of 7,000 people across 150 countries. Its goal is to ensure a healthier future for all the world's people. To accomplish this, it works closely with governments and others. It released a study revealing the number of Iraqi civilian deaths.

Bibliography of Books

Michael C. C. Adams, *Living Hell: The Dark Side of the Civil War*. Baltimore, MD: Johns Hopkins University Press, 2016.

Yervant Alexanian, *Forced into Genocide: Memoirs of an Armenian Soldier in the Ottoman Turkish Army*, ed. Adrienne G. Alexanian. New Brunswick, NJ: Transaction, 2017.

Scott Anderson, *Fractured Lands: How the Arab World Came Apart*. New York, NY: Anchor Books/Penguin Random House, 2017.

Eliott Behar, *Tell It to the World: International Justice and the Secret Campaign to Hide Mass Murder in Kosovo*. Toronto, Canada: Dundum Press, 2014.

Alex J. Bellamy, *Massacres and Morality: Mass Atrocities in an Age of Civil Immunity*. Oxford, UK: Oxford University Press, 2014.

Doris L. Bergen, *War and Genocide: A Concise History of the Holocaust*, 3rd ed. Lanham, MD: Rowman & Littlefield, 2016.

Neta C. Crawford, *Accountability for Killing: Moral Responsibility for Collateral Damage in America's Post-9/11 Wars*. New York, NY: Oxford University Press, 2015.

David M. Crowe, *War Crimes, Genocide, and Justice: A Global History*. New York, NY: Palgrave Macmillan, 2014.

Claire Garbett, *The Concept of the Civilian: Legal Recognition, Adjudication and the Trials of International Criminal Justice*. Oxon, UK, and New York, NY: Routledge, 2015.

Habtu Ghebre-Ab, *Massacre at Wekidiba: The Tragic Story of a Village in Eritrea*. Trenton, NJ: Red Sea Press, 2013.

Rebecca Gordon, *American Nuremberg: The U.S. Officials Who Should Stand Trial for Post-9/11 War Crimes.* New York, NY: Hot Books/Skyhorse Publishing, 2016.

A. C. Grayling, *Among the Dead Cities: Is the Targeting of Civilians in War Ever Justified?* New York, NY: Bloomsbury Academic, 2014.

Robert Howse, Hélène Ruiz-Fabri, Geir Ulfstein, and Michelle Q. Zang, editors, *The Legitimacy of International Trade Courts and Tribunals.* New York, NY: Cambridge University Press, 2018.

Adam Jones, *Genocide: A Comprehensive Introduction*, 3rd ed. Oxon, UK, and New York, NY: Routledge, 2017.

Howard Jones, *My Lai: Vietnam, 1968, and the Descent into Darkness.* New York, NY: Oxford University Press, 2017.

Mei Ju-Ao, *The Tokyo Trial and War Crimes in Asia.* Basingstoke, UK: Palgrave Macmillan, 2018.

Sebastian Kaempf, *Saving Soldiers or Civilians?: Casualty Aversion vs. Civilian Protection in Asymmetric Conflicts.* Cambridge, UK: Cambridge University Press, 2018.

Shima D. Keene, *Lethal and Legal: The Effects of Drone Strikes.* Carlisle, PA: Strategic Studies Institute and U.S. Army War College Press, 2016.

Barthomiej Krzan, *Prosecuting International Crimes: A Multidisciplinary Approach.* Leiden, Belgium: Martinus Nijhoff, 2016.

Frank Ledwidge, *Investment in Blood: The True Cost of Britain's Afghan War.* New Haven, CT: Yale University Press, 2013.

Larry Lewis and Diane M. Vavrichek, *Rethinking the Drone War: National Security, Legitimacy and Civilian Casualties in U.S. Counterterrorism Operations.* Quantico, VA: Marine Corps University Press, 2017.

Nick McDonnell, *Solatia: An Account of Civilian Casualties in America's Wars.* New York, NY: Blue Rider Press/Penguin, 2018.

Norman M. Naimark, *Genocide: A World History.* New York, NY: Oxford University Press, 2017.

Damien Rogers, *Law, Politics and the Limits of Prosecuting Mass Atrocity.* New York, NY: Palgrave Macmillan, 2017.

Frederik Rosén, *Collateral Damage: Candid History of a Peculiar Form of Death.* London, UK: Hurst, 2016.

Marcus Schulzke, *Just War Theory and Civilian Casualties: Protecting the Victims of War.* Cambridge, UK: Cambridge University Press, 2017.

Taylor B. Seybolt, Jay D. Aronson, and Baruch Fischoff, editors, *Counting Civilian Casualties: An Introduction to Recording and Estimating Nonmilitary Deaths in Conflict.* New York, NY: Oxford University Press, 2013.

Krysten Sinema, *Who Must Die in Rwanda's Genocide?* Lanham, MD: Lexington Books, 2015.

Amrit Singh, *Death by Drone.* New York, NY: Open Society Foundations, 2015.

Thomas W. Smith, *Human Rights and War Through Civilian Eyes.* Philadelphia, PA: University of Pennsylvania Press, 2017.

Index